Are *You*
Being Told What to
Believe?

Are *You* Being Told What to *Believe?*

How important is what we believe?

By Ruth Beebe

ISBN: 978-1-4269-3983-9 (soft)
ISBN: 978-1-4269-3984-6 (ebook)

*Our mission is to efficiently provide the world's finest, most comprehensive
book publishing service, enabling every author to experience success.
To find out how to publish your book, your way, and have it available
worldwide, visit us online at www.trafford.com*

Trafford rev. 8/17/2010

 www.trafford.com

North America & international
toll-free: 1 888 232 4444 (USA & Canada)
phone: 250 383 6864 ♦ fax: 812 355 4082

Table of Contents

Preface

Have you ever stopped to consider just what your beliefs actually are, or where these beliefs came from? Do you believe in evolution for example? What if evolution is in fact nothing more than scientific *theory* or *speculation*? What if there was really no scientific evidence what so ever for evolution? Would you still believe? If so why? Because we were all taught in school that we evolved? If it is taught in school than it must be the truth…right? But is it?

Have you ever stopped to consider why God is not allowed in school or other public places? Better yet, have you ever noticed that the only *God* not allowed in school is the Christian God? Have you ever wondered why? Think about it for a moment, Witchcraft, Pagan beliefs, even Allah is allowed in our public schools yet there can be no mention of the Christian God on whom the United States of America was founded! Don't you ever wonder why?

Like it or not…believe it or not, we are all being told what to think and believe every single day of our lives! Our minds, our thoughts are being manipulated!

I was raised in some unusual beliefs. Although my grandfather brought a strong vein of Christianity into our family there were also elements of the occult present for as long as I can remember. I have to say that I genuinely believe that God has been guiding my steps my entire life. I believe that I have a purpose and a big part of that purpose is this book. All of my life my steps have been guided through places where information of various kinds was made available to me. For example; I remember seeing a documentary in a high school history class that no one else I know remembers seeing. It was about WW2 and how the good ole USA tested it's new A Bomb. Basically, we went to a small inhabited island, the natives of which had likely never seen a white man, let alone huge ships and aircraft, and told them that we wanted to test our new weapon on their island in the name of world peace. They agreed and we proceeded to blow them off the face of the earth! Yep, we killed them all! Not only do I remember the documentary, I also remember the class, it was a high school history class (10th grade, I think) and the name of my teacher. I remember this vividly, probably because it was the beginning of my basic distrust of the US government. After all, if our government is capable of slaughtering hundreds of peaceful natives for a weapon, what else are they capable of?

I mention this here because it is important to the theme of the book, I don't know what the name of this little propaganda documentary is, nor even if it still exists. I am sure that there is someone out there who remembers it also. Please bear with me.

In my 20s I began to hear reports of bio-weapon and nuclear tests being done on US citizens not to mention MK Ultra, the US/Canadian mind control experiments of the 60s and 70s. Of course who can forget the subliminal messages placed in movies and TV shows back in the 70s? Do you really think that blind trust is merited?

Having been introduced to some occult practices at a young age gave me an unusual perspective as well as an interest in things such as; UFOs, gods and goddesses, giants and of course science fiction!

I have also, always had a keen interest in the truth! I hate being lied to!

Many years ago I prayed to God to show me the truth about the world. Be careful what you ask for you might get it!

The more research I did, the more I realized how many of these very different seeming things are actually connected and actually guided!

Each and every day we are bombarded with images and information. Often the information presented to us is portrayed as factual. Sometimes it is presented as scientific evidence,

But what if the facts or evidence presented to us is wrong? What if in fact, this information is nothing more than scientific theory or speculation or worse the deliberate manipulation of your thoughts and beliefs?

Of course this couldn't really happen…could it? Believe it or not it can and does happen every single day.

Did you know that more than 80% of all Americans believe in UFOs? Many of these believe that they have seen a UFO and many of these believe that they have been abducted by Aliens! What if these accounts are real? A better question yet is what if they have always been here? Could it be possible that these beings might be mentioned in the Bible?

The information in this book is strictly based on my own research and the connections I make are my own opinion. It is not my intention to convince anyone of anything. Nor are all of my sources necessarily verifiable. Informational web sites which provide *uncomfortable* information frequently disappear from public view but a few well chosen searches might bring you some interesting results! I fully realize that people will accept and believe only what they want to, so I will not try and convince you of anything. However it IS my intention to change your perspective, just a little.

I am a Christian and this book is from a Christian perspective. All of these things mentioned in this book are connected and all are part of a greater agenda, to destroy God and you! Make no mistake this is a spiritual battle with just one goal to destroy humanity.

I hope that this book opens your eyes to a somewhat different perspective of reality. This is the one and only focus of this book. May God bless you in your own search!

Are You Being Told What To Believe?

Are you being told what to think? Are you being told what to believe? How important are our beliefs? Most of us don't really give a lot of thought to how our beliefs impact the world around us or to what our beliefs really mean to us. I hope to show you in this book how vitally important your beliefs really are.

I also wish to examine popular beliefs and show you not only how all of these things are connected, but how your beliefs are being controlled! It is extremely important for everyone to take charge of your minds, your thoughts and beliefs because if you don't someone else will!

We all have things that we believe or believe in. We can believe in ourselves or others, we can believe in our point of view (at least until it is proven incorrect). You can believe in happiness or that the world is a dark and terrible place. You can believe in God, or Krishna or evolution.

Belief sets are almost as unique as the individual.

So how important is this? Does it really matter what we believe?

What you believe matters SO much that people are spending billions upon billions of dollars to gain control of what you think and believe AND this has been ongoing for decades!

Have you ever really given any thought to the theory of evolution for example? Did you know that it has absolutely no scientific merit? There is not one single shred of evidence to prove that evolution ever took place, I am of course talking about macro evolution here, micro evolution or evolution within a species happens all of the time, but macro evolution, the concept of one species turning into another has never ever been witnessed nor is there any kind of proof in existence for it! Yet there are actual laws in existence to protect it AND it is the only scientific theory *ever* to be protected by law! Stop and let that sink in for a minute.

WHY do you think this is?

Have you ever stopped to consider why the only GOD that is being denied a place in public areas (like government buildings and *schools*) is the God of the Bible? Stop and think about this for a minute, You can have witchcraft, Satanism, the gods and goddesses of mythology, Allah and evolution (yes this is a religion, more further on) Yet not one single Christian word can be spoken! Have you ever stopped to wonder how this can happen in a country founded on Christian values? Or, WHY?

I mean there has been a lot of hoopla about removing God from public areas, citing that religion has no place in a democratic country, but apparently the only *religion* considered offensive is Christianity. Have you ever wondered why? Did you know that approximately 80% of Americans believe in UFOs?

Did you know that there are literally dozens of gods and goddesses being worshiped throughout the world today and yes that includes the good old USA! In fact the worship of the deities of old is making an amazing come back! You can in fact go on-line right now and find a site that will tell you how to build an altar to Baal. Yes this would be the same Baal or Baal's (Baal basically means lord and is usually followed by another name) that people in ancient Egypt sacrificed their babies to, by burning them alive at his altar! The fact of the matter is that when you remove Christianity from the picture it opens the door to all kinds of possibilities!

There will be things in this book that will upset and offend some people and I apologize for this up front, but until you understand what exactly you are up against you have no way of protecting yourself, so you really need to know! I will not claim that I know everything or that I have all of the answers, I don't believe that anyone does, all I ask is that you take the time to do some research for yourself, the truth is readily available to anyone who chooses to look for it, at least at the time of this writing, no guarantees in the near future since sites keep disappearing from the internet daily, especially those that hit too close to home or those that aren't easily discredited. Please do yourself a favor and take the time to do the research! I cannot even begin to tell you how vitally important this is to you and to the people you love!

My goal here is to examine the various beliefs in the public domain today and show you how these things are connected. Many of these things seem unrelated but are actually either very related or are actually the same thing with a different spin.

I will tell you right up front that I am a Christian and yes I do see things from a Christian perspective but this hasn't always been the case. In fact I began the research for this book before I fell in love with Jesus Christ, but Christian or not this book is very pertinent to you! What you don't know will cost you very dearly! Did you know that Christians are actually dying for their beliefs in some parts of the world? Did you know that the US government holds many patents on mind control methods? If so, have you ever wondered how they tested them?

Has it occurred to you to wonder why so many people are dying lately? Or why there is so much cancer or diabetes? Have you noticed that it is getting difficult these days to find anyone over 50 who are not on some kind of life-time medication(s)? These things keep getting more and more prevalent and hardly anyone even thinks to question why this is happening! This is a curiosity unto itself. Do you find that you have difficulty thinking straight? Are you finding that your memory is not so great lately? Have you noticed that this is a fairly common thing with people these days? Have you ever wondered why?

These may not seem like very important questions, but they are!

There was a story on the internet a while back about how the bees are disappearing. This is actually pretty serious, if you stop and think about what bees actually do, our food crops rely on bees for pollination. The story also appeared on TV (I want to say 60 minutes but I'm not sure) anyway the story is that cell phones are responsible for the loss of bee populations. I believe this is true, but only in part, believe it or not the same thing that is responsible for your difficulty in thinking is the same thing that is playing a major role in the reduction of bees and its not good news for any of us!

I know that there are going to be people who will not believe or want to believe some or even most of this book, this is your choice, and I know that there will be people who will try very hard to discredit not only me but any or all information in this book, it is to be expected.

It is not my goal to frighten people, it is not my goal to anger people, nor is it my goal to convince anyone of anything. The truth is that (at least for the moment) we all have free will (thank you Lord!) and no one can be convinced to believe anything that they don't want to believe!

My goal here, my one and only goal is to plant some seeds in your mind to get you started on a search for your own answers, to wake you up to the possibility that things are not what they seem and hopefully get you to look at things in a different light, because it's later than you think!

Some of the things that I want to discuss in this book are; the very popular *law of attraction,* evolution vs. creation, gods and goddesses, UFOs, Aliens and angels, Who is really running the world and their agenda, scare/control tactics and of course Christianity and how all of these are connected.

Believe it or not they are connected and they all directly affect *every human being on this planet!*

How important is what we believe?

You are being told what to think and believe every day, does it matter? Only if your immortal soul matters to you!

Evolution vs. Creation?

Are you being told what to think?

I think that this is the best place to start because it was the introduction to the *theory* of evolution that started the ball rolling, so to speak on what is happening today.

I seriously doubt that there is anyone anymore that hasn't at least heard of the theory of evolution. Basically put, the theory of evolution states that (I am not sure of the time line here, it keeps changing) millions or billions of years ago there was rock and rain and the rain beat on the rock which formed the so-called primordial soup. In this *soup* amino acids formed which caused/enabled single cell organisms to appear, which evolved into more complex creatures and eventually mammals crawled out of the mire and became man and of course this process also accounts for all of the other life forms on earth including the ape from which modern man supposedly evolved. Probably not the best description of evolution, I suppose that if you are really unfamiliar with this it wouldn't be hard to pick up a book, but for the purpose of this book it's good enough, the basics are covered. The first thing that I would like to point out here is that there is not one single shred of scientific evidence that macro evolution (the theory of one species developing from another) ever occurred, the science, the *real* science points to creation. Not only to creation but to the Biblical account of creation! Oh, I am sure that evolutionists would gladly provide you with ample so-called examples which are supposed to be proof that supports their beliefs, but the truth is that the data or evidence supports a young earth (approximately 6000 years), a young universe, a global flood and the coexistence of man and dinosaur living together at the same point in history.

Evolutionists will try to provide data or evidence which supports their theories, but (at least in my opinion) it always seems weak compared to the creation evidence. Unfortunately, most evolutionists, instead of accepting that the evidence supports creation, will instead, think up new ways to explain the evidence in an attempt to bend the evidence to fit their beliefs! Folks, when you believe in something despite the lack of data or facts to support your belief, it is called faith, which makes Darwinian evolution a religion! No matter how you look at it, it is still a religion! I am sure that there are many evolutionists that will argue this fact, but consider this: If believing in God or Jesus Christ or any other deity for that matter without actual rock solid evidence to back it up makes your belief system a religion, then can't the same thing be said of evolutionary beliefs? Bending data to fit your beliefs is an act of faith, is it not? Therefore the logical conclusion (it seems to me) has to be that evolution for many scientists and others, is their religion!

There are a great number of scientists today who started their careers as evolutionists and became Christians (or at least creationists) when they discovered the scientific evidence. Did you know that there is a layer of sediment deposit called the Austin chalk that runs throughout the entire world that occurred as a result of a world-wide flood? Sound familiar? Not only does this layer exist throughout the entire world, there are also millions of fossils in this layer that indicate death by suffocation, consistent with the Biblical flood account. In fact, not only is there evidence of a world-wide flood, the scientific facts and findings in general are indicative of a *young* Earth and of intelligent *design*! The scientific data points to a designer.....a *CREATOR*!

Evolutionary scientists like to refer to the geologic column as evidence of an ancient world basically it is layers upon layers of various deposits that supposedly span millions and millions of years. But if this column actually does represent millions of years, then how can you possibly have a fossilized tree growing up through the layers? Have you ever heard of a tree with a million year life span? Especially when you stop and consider that the oldest living thing on Earth is a either an Irish Oak or a Bristlecone pine tree dated at 4,500 to 4,767 years old, which is consistent with the Biblical flood account.

Yet, many people cling to this belief that we all *just appeared* rather than accept the possibility that there could be an actual *creator*. WHY? Why would intelligent people believe in something that has only fabricated or assigned data to back it up, when there is literally mountains of evidence to the contrary? When the actual evidence points to God?

I suppose that there are different reasons but mostly I think that they just don't want to be accountable to a creator. At any rate, it always seems to me that the people who proclaim evolution the loudest seem angry and cynical.

Perhaps it is fear, or some kind of status thinking, I don't know.

So, what's the big deal anyway, why does it matter that evolution is taught in school while any mention of God is not allowed?

Keep in mind that the theory of evolution has been proven false by a myriad of scientists, yet it is still taught as fact in our schools! WHY? Did you know that Charles Darwin himself said that if anyone were to prove that the cell was anything more than a blob of protein that his theory would be worthless? Guess what? A human cell is a lot more than a blob of protein! It is actually closer to a tiny city constantly moving with activity.

Quoting from the book 'Evolution a Theory in Crisis', by Michael Denton, molecular biologist. pages 328–329. "To grasp the reality of life as it has been revealed by molecular biology, we must magnify a cell a thousand million times until it is twenty kilometers in diameter and resembles a giant airship large enough to cover a great city like London or New York. What we would then see would be an object of unparalleled complexity and adaptive design.

On the surface of the cell we would see millions of openings, like the port holes of a vast space ship, opening and closing to allow a continual stream of materials in and out. If we were to enter one of these openings we would find ourselves in a world of supreme technology and bewildering complexity. We would see endless highly organized corridors and conduits branching in every direction away from the perimeter of the cell, some leading to the central memory bank in the nucleus and others to assembly plants and processing units."

"The nucleus itself would be a vast spherical chamber more than a kilometer in diameter, resembling a geodesic dome inside of which we would see, all neatly stacked together in ordered arrays, the miles of coiled chains of the DNA molecules.

"We would wonder at the level of control implicit in the movement of so many objects down so many seemingly endless conduits, all in prefect unison. We would see all around us, in every direction we looked, all sorts of robot like machines. We would notice that the simplest of the functional components of the cell, the protein molecules, were astonishingly complex pieces of molecular machinery, each one consisting of about three thousand atoms arranged in highly organized 3-D spatial conformation.

We wonder even more as we watched the strangely purposeful activities of these weird molecular machines, particularly when we realize that, despite all our accumulated knowledge of physics and chemistry, the task of designing one such molecular machine-that is one single functional protein molecule-would be beyond our capacity ... Yet the life of the cell depends on the integrated activities of thousands, certainly tens and probably hundreds of thousands of different protein molecules"

Pretty amazing statement wouldn't you say? Of course, this is only one example, the list of goes on and on. The eye, for example, is so complex that even Charles Darwin himself could not come up with any kind of explanation for it! And this was just one eye, to take this one step farther and note that we not only have two eyes but that they work together with the function of the brain makes this even more amazing!

So why exactly, is this extremely flawed theory still being taught as fact? Maybe, because it undermines the very foundation of the Bible! If the Biblical account of creation is wrong then it calls into question everything else in the Bible. Add to this, that neither God nor any scientific data which supports creation is allowed in our schools and what do you get?

It is very important that you make this connection because it is the foundation which makes the enslavement of humanity possible! This is the cornerstone of the new world order it all begins with a lie, presented as fact. Have you noticed that if you want to worship Allah in school, or participate in the practices of paganism it is perfectly fine, just don't mention God, or Jesus Christ!

This is not an accident this is by design, everything according to plan!

I will say this once again, do not take my word for it, please do your own research!

So what are some other problems of evolutionary theory? Wow, where to begin, there are so many!

Let's begin with the math. According to the creation account if you go back to the flood of Noah, there were 8 people left on earth after the flood with a growth rate of 2.5% (which is a conservative growth rate) the current population of earth today would be 6.5 billion people, which is right on the mark!

Evolution however, give mans origins as being 500,000 years ago, this date at a growth rate of 2.5% would result in a population of 2.45 x 10 to the 990 power. This is more people than there are electrons in the entire universe! Even if you reduce the age of man to 100,000 years with a .1% growth rate you still end up with far more people than would fit on planet earth and this is just people, it doesn't take into account animals, birds or fish! People have tried to make this number work but no matter how hard they try they just can't arrive at the current world population starting with a time-line of anything greater than 4500 years!

This is just the math, their problems don't stop here!

According to evolutionists man and dinosaur were not on the earth at the same time, that we were actually separated by millions of years, yet we have foot prints of dinosaurs with human footprints in them. Evolutionists like to say that well there must be some means by which these earlier layers have been softened (science knows of no method by which this could happen) and then man could leave footprints. OK, fair enough, then how do they explain the dinosaur footprints found that show a dinosaurs footprint on/over that of a man? Both of these have been discovered, sounds like pretty solid evidence for man and dinosaur living together to me!

Of course it is about what we believe, is it not? Man has always tried to make the facts fit his own theories I guess it is just a matter of getting people to believe you! This approach worked for Hitler and a few others over the years. I guess if you can get people to believe it, it's true! Therein lies the problem!

How important is what we believe?

In a book that I recently read Creation or Evolution, Does it Really Matter What You Believe? Pg 47 the following statement is made: "As long as evolutionists keep their conceptions as vague abstractions, they can sound plausible. But when rigorous mathematics is applied to their generalities, and their assertions are specifically quantified, the underpinnings of Darwinian evolution are exposed as so implausible and unrealistic as to be impossible."

Even some of the smallest things on earth, bacteria are so complex that to suggest that they somehow just 'appeared' on earth (not taking into account the systems needed for their survival) is ludicrous!

Yet over and over again we are told that evolution is true scientific fact! Nothing could be further from the truth! To be quite honest the belief in Darwinian evolution requires so much blind faith that this could only be classified as a religion! Many of the faithful followers of which, rival the most devout zealots of any religion in history! Yet this is taught as *scientific fact* in every public class room in many countries! WHY?

One argument that people like to make is, the carbon 14 theory.

http://www.earthage.org/radio/carbon14.htm

At this link you will find not only this quote but some other excellent information on radio dating as well:

What About Carbon-14

- "The Carbon-14 method of dating can be used to date things that were once living such as wood, animal skins, tissue, and bones (provided they are not mineralized). Due to the short half-life (5,730 years) of Carbon-14, this method can only be used to date things that are less than 50,000 years old (max). And though some evolutionists claim that it is accurate up to 40,000 years,[1] in reality it is highly unreliable for anything over 5,000 years old.

For example, roughly half of the dates produced by this method are rejected by archeologists as being either too far off or impossible.[2] Those who think it is accurate beyond 5,000 years should know that C-14 has been used to date over 20 different <u>Dinosaur Bones</u> and other <u>Artifacts</u> associated with dinosaurs (such as <u>wood</u> and <u>trees</u> from Axel Heiberg Island, and coal), [3,4,5,6] and in every case ages of between 9,800 and 50,000 years were obtained. Other methods of radiometric dating require the use of various unverifiable assumptions and are also, for that reason (and <u>various others</u>), highly questionable."

For those who wonder why dates that are older than 6,000 years are often obtained by this method, consider the words of Sylvia Baker:

- *"Many crucial objections cast doubt on the reliability of this method. We shall consider just two of them.*

  1. The theory assumes that carbon-14 is in equilibrium in the atmosphere -- that it is being broken down at the same rate at which it is being produced. However, calculations made to test this assumption suggest that carbon-14 is being produced nearly one third faster than it is disintegrating. If this is true, then none of the fossils that have been dated by this method could be more than a few thousand years old..."

- *2.... It is also true that cosmic rays would have been deflected away from the earth most effectively by the earth's magnetic field if, as we have argued, this was much stronger in the past. With fewer cosmic rays reaching the atmosphere, there would have been less production of carbon-14 then than now.*

- *Thus we have seen that evolutionists have no really reliable method of dating fossils..."* 7

Furthermore, the Carbon-14 dates for dinosaur bones (and carbonized wood associated with dino strata) are in serious conflict with the purported 65 million year "date" for their extinction. This presents a problem for evolution, and the Geological Time Chart itself, especially since the possibility of contamination from surrounding soil was eliminated. In addition, many of the samples were sent to different labs for comparison dating. Yet, in spite of these facts, when a mammoth or Neanderthal bone is "dated" at <u>35,000 years</u> it is accepted as fact and proclaimed widely in popular publications, while similarly preserved (i.e. un-fossilized) dinosaur bones, (yielding similar dates) are scoffed at by evolution *believers* and/or ignored by virtually all supposedly objective "science" publications: I.E. those that are still covering for the virtually bankrupt theory of evolution, and whose editors are so filled with Pride that they don't even want to look at the evidence before them, much less admit the very likely possibility that they were wrong.

The conclusion by many scientists and others who are aware of this is that radiometric dating methods are nothing more than guesses that are based more on highly speculative theories rather than on facts, and that it is very likely that

Dinosaurs did not become extinct 65 million years ago, as we have been told (over and over and over again) by the mass media, but rather in the recent past. Perhaps that's why two of them are described in detail on the <u>Old Testament book of Job</u>, and why numerous artifacts that clearly depict them (i.e. the <u>Ica Stones</u>) have been found at archeological sites in Mexico and South America."

<u>http://www.earthage.org/EarthOldorYoung/Radiometric %20Dating,%20and%20The%20Age%20of%20the%20 Earth.htm</u>

Of course from this actual link you will be able to explore the evidence in much more detail. This is an excellent site, I highly recommend it!

Evolutionists like to claim that the world is billions of years old, but is it really? In my search:

"Earths geomagnetic field, young earth evidence (dog pile search engine)"

I found numerous links to creation and evolutionary debates about Young earth theory. I recommend that you do your own search you will be presented with both sides of the debate.

I know that as a Christian I am biased in the creation direction, but I honestly think that even if I weren't biased I would still find the creation science much stronger and more compelling and more honest in the respect that there are many scientists today who began their careers as evolutionists and became creationists and even Christians due to their own scientific findings! To my mind this is a far more honest approach then trying to form the evidence to support your beliefs.

I can't help but wonder though how many evolutionists realize how old (and religious) their beliefs are? Did you know that you can find an interesting reference to similar beliefs in the Bible?

Jeremiah 2:27

Who say to a tree, 'You are my father,' And to a stone, 'You gave me birth'.

This sounds a lot like Darwinian evolution to me! Of course this is simplified and is basically talking about idolatry but the idea is very similar.

The concept of evolution is actually nothing new the idea has been around a long time. Even the world's great thinkers such as Plato and Socrates explored and rejected the idea of evolution a long time ago! It does make me wonder, why humanity will return over and over again to such a flawed idea just so that they do not have to accept that there is a God!? Why are people so fearful that there might actually be a God? If God is love then what do we have to fear? Have you ever wondered this?

OK, so what other problems does evolution have? What about the age of the Earths geomagnetic field?

The Earths geomagnetic field was first measured in 1829 and numerous studies have been done since. The basic findings are that the Earths geomagnetic field is reducing by half every 1400 years. Basically what this means is that if you go back in time, the Earths geomagnetic field is doubling in strength every 1400 years. So if you go backwards in time, 10,000 years ago the Earths geomagnetic field would have been so strong that no living thing could have survived! This basically means that, once again, the Biblical account of creation has been confirmed.

However, evolutionists counter with the precept that the Earths geomagnetic field has not been constant, that it does in fact fluctuate and that there are periodic reversals. OK, even if this is true it still has to be taken as a 'stand alone' type of data and it still doesn't change the fact that more and more data is coming to light which confirms creation! Nor for that matter does it actually prove that the earth is not exactly the age that creationists believe it to be! In other words it doesn't disprove the age of the geomagnetic field.

What about the scientific findings of the mitochondrial Adam and Eve? These are the scientific findings that we all descended from the same two people? Some scientists like to speculate that this took place 10,000 to 20,000 years ago, but there are also a large group of scientists who actually believe this date to be 6,000 to 10,000 years ago.

Of course, you need to *always* keep in mind the motives of people presenting information. If it seems to you that information is being presented as a means by which to keep you confused, then it just might be exactly that!

This is why you need to ask God for guidance when you are researching information, so that you can see the truth for yourself! Keep in mind that the Bible says that the deceptions of the end times will be such as to fool even the elect if that were possible!

Matthew 24:24

For there shall arise false Christ's, and false prophets, and shall show great signs and wonders; so as to lead astray, if possible, even the elect.

I do realize that we are not talking about false Christ's and false prophets here, but we *ARE* talking about a belief system, and like it or not, evolution is a religion!

Not only is evolution a religion but it is a religion which is bent on destroying God, Jesus and any belief therein!

To understand this fact, you only need to look at evolutionary response to anyone proclaiming to be a Christian! Many evolutionists show a tendency to look at Christians (and/or creationists) as being ignorant or unenlightened and weak. To these people anyone who *needs* a creator to cling to must be a weak superstitious fool! They are so sure of their own superiority of beliefs that they cannot even conceive of the idea that maybe, just maybe, these *weak* people might actually see something that they don't (or don't want to see). Science is their God and it doesn't matter that it isn't necessarily telling them what they want to hear, but just like many religious leaders in the past, who bent the words of the Bible to match their beliefs they bend the data to fit their theories!

How much different are these people really from any of these religious leaders who committed similar acts? Isn't science *supposed* to be about the actual facts? Yet far too often it isn't! I suppose that to some degree this is human nature but I really do think that if ones religion is evolution, that they should recognize this fact!

I would like to ask the evolutionist's one question. Do your beliefs make you happy?

Most Christians have a deep and profound sense of joy and happiness which comes from a relationship with God. The scientific evidence for creation only adds to this joy because it is just further proof of God's undying love.

Can evolutionists truly find joy in the belief that there is no God, no hope, no freedom and that only death awaits them? I tend to believe NO! In fact, it seems to me that the loudest of the evolutionary leaders seem cynical and cold in their beliefs. Do these people just not want to be happy? This is the impression that I get, but who knows!

How important is what we believe?

The bottom line is this: We are being told that evolution is fact when it is anything but fact! Unfortunately, the teaching of evolution as fact has a major impact on our thinking and our beliefs.

If there is no God, then there is no accountability. Don't you find it interesting that since the introduction of evolution as scientific fact, the number of serial killers has grown at such a rate that we rarely even hear any mention of them through any news media? Some serial killers have even said that if there really was a God they may have never started killing in the first place! Think about that for a minute!

And is it really just a coincidence that since God was removed from school and evolution and paganism welcomed, that we suddenly have kids bringing guns and knives to school to kill each other? Think this is just a coincidence?

What was that quote? "If you tell a child that he is an animal, then don't be surprised when he acts like one"!

Interesting quote but it really doesn't stop there, does it?!

First you introduce the emptiness of evolution, then you remove God or any mention of God, Jesus or even a creator, then you introduce the darkness of the seductive *magic* aspect of the occult type of belief and now you have children that are ready to be molded to believe what they are told to believe! Isn't that just amazing!? What? It never occurred to you that there could be a connection?

Folks, this is not a new concept, it becomes a lot easier to invade a country if you first win the minds of the children!

How important is what we believe?

Of course this is just my opinion!

So I ask you, does it really matter what you think? Does it matter what you believe? Does it matter what the children believe? You might not think so, but I guarantee you that there are a lot of very powerful people in this world who care very much what you and your children believe and they spend a lot of time and money to this end! If you don't take charge of what you believe, somebody else will!

If you have the notion in your head that Christianity is an outdated or antiquated religion, or that Christianity is somehow evil or set on your destruction, then you really need to take a much closer look at why you believe this.

Keep in mind that the same people who are trying to destroy God are the ones who are dragging you and your children into the darkness of empty beliefs. Why do they need to destroy God or Christianity unless it is somehow a threat to their plans? AND Christianity is the *ONLY* religion that is under full scale attack throughout the entire world!

Keep these questions in mind and I will try to connect more of the dots for you. It is my hope that by the end of this book you will be able to see the world around you in a different light. Maybe the world is not what you believe it to be!

Gods and Goddesses

Are you being told what to think?

It is interesting how accepting our society in general has become of gods and goddesses in our culture lately.

Now before anyone starts going off on censorship, let me just say this; I *used* to be against censorship too, until I realized that censorship is already going on and the ONLY thing being censored today, is GOD! In a society that *claims* to value freedom of speech and freedom of religion everyone *should* be able to think, speak and believe according to their personal sense of what's what! So why exactly is it that Jesus Christ, the faith that the good old USA was founded on is being censored? So let me say that if you are going to use the censorship card on me you had better be willing to accept the fact that I have every right to my beliefs! At least for the moment!

23

That being said let me also say that I have always been a sci-fi/ fantasy fan. It's just so much fun, isn't it? To wander off into fantastic unexplored realms, seeking whatever grand adventure awaits us?!

Lately though I am seeing a trend that concerns me. Especially taken with a lot of other things, that don't appear related but put together are.

With movies, TV shows, video games and yes even cartoons promoting nearly every form of god and goddess, aliens, magic, sorcery, witchcraft etc. as fun or entertainment what chance does the average kid today have? The question that I keep coming back to over and over again is this; how many of these children are actually exposed to God or Jesus Christ? How many are actually introduced to the beauty and truth of faith? For that matter how many adults ever stop and think about what's going into their minds? Did you know that the average child is exposed to 12,000 simulated murders by the age of 14? Yet, there had better be no mention of God or morals in public schools! Then we wonder why we have children murdering children!

So why is it that every child in America can be exposed to every other alternate religion in the world, yet cannot even hear a word about the one *real* God? Do you think that this just worked out this way? Maybe you think that this happened because of some disgruntled atheist!

Guess what? It is all planned and has been ongoing for a long time, the plan itself actually started kicking in about 60 years ago (give or take). None of this just happened, nor is it necessarily just apathy on the part of Americans. After all, it's hard to take a stand when you are having difficulty thinking straight, and this too is part of the plan!

As I mentioned in the previous chapter, this all began with the introduction of the theory of evolution and how we have progressed! Now we have witchcraft in the schoolroom, and not a peep about God!!! A little too interesting, wouldn't you say?

You might be able to say coincidence if it actually stopped there, but it doesn't. I hope that by the end of this book you will see what the powers that be are trying so very hard to keep you from seeing, that this is all carefully planned and who or what is doing the planning!

I have always thought that the gods and goddesses of ancient religions were an interesting subject, but a few years back during research into these beings it occurred to me that they might have actually existed and were not just mere mythology. It seems to be a popular idea that Hercules was a real person. Hercules was supposed to be half human, half god. He is often portrayed as a hero, but in many stories he was quite insane, went on rampages and murdered people, etc. I can't help but wonder how he was immortalized as a hero?!

Anyway, in the Bible, it says; Genesis 6:4 There were giants in the earth in those days; and also after that, when the sons of God came in unto the daughters of men and they bare children to them, the same became mighty men which were of old, men of renown. (Some Bibles say gods of old, and give them the name Nephilim)

This is a very popular quote for UFO believers, I know, I thought we were talking about gods and goddesses. Just bear with me it IS connected!

The UFO/ alien movement (for lack of a better word) likes to point to this passage in the Bible as proof that aliens have been visiting earth and genetically altering us in some supposedly beneficial way. Unfortunately what they always seem to leave out is the fact that this event corrupted humanity so badly that God destroyed the earth! The very next chapter starts telling about Gods plan to destroy the earth! So these people might want to take a look at what came next!

Yes, I do believe that something happened here that produced unnatural offspring. It does make sense that this was in fact the union of fallen angels with man that resulted in gigantic beings. In the Bible after the serpent deceived Eve into eating the forbidden fruit, God is angry and says to Satan, Genesis 3:15 "And I will put enmity between thee and the woman, and between thy seed and her seed; it shall bruise thy head and thou shall bruise his heal." Yes I do understand the reference to Jesus Christ here and I know that this is generally understood differently by many Christian groups however there is a point to be made about the reference to Satan's *seed* here!

It does seem to indicate that Satan (and other fallen angels?) can indeed produce offspring! This seems to imply physical offspring, not just spiritual offspring. There has been a lot of speculation about the methods thereof, but unnatural offspring as a result of human/angel union definitely seems to be the result.

We know that giants were real because grave sites have been unearthed of beings that ranged from 9 to 12 feet in height! Although I don't remember where I read this, I do remember reading that the DNA of some of these beings did not match any human DNA on earth. This was however at least 10 or 12 years ago and I just do not remember the specifics.

Giants appear in the folklore of nearly every culture on the face of the earth. Giants were almost always cruel and evil and although worshiped were known to consume humans as food. If you really doubt that giants actually existed let me recommend a site for you www.biblebelievers.org.au/giants.htm this site should give you an idea of how big these beings really were! I should mention here that accounts can be found of giants up to 200 feet tall! Although I know of no such archaeological finds. In an excerpt from; www.mysteriousworld.com/Journal/2003/Spring/Giants/.

"However, whereas some giants are perceived as gently and harmless, even beneficent, more often than not, giants were described as being possessed of wicked minds and insatiable appetites – engaging in unnatural acts shocking even to the modern mind. These wicked sons of Belial were known for their immense size, raging appetites, devious minds, aggressive behavior, technological sophistication and above all, skill in the art of war!"

And one more; "The origin of the Nephilim begins with a story of fallen angels. Shemhazai, an angel of high rank, led a sect of angels in a descent to earth to instruct humans in righteousness. The tutelage went on for a few centuries, but soon the angels pined for human females. After lusting, the fallen angels instructed the women in magic and conjuring, mated with them, and produced hybrid offspring: the Nephilim. The Nephilim were gigantic in stature. Their strength was prodigious and their appetites immense. Upon devouring all of humankind's resources, they began to consume humans themselves. The Nephilim attacked and oppressed humans and were the cause of massive destruction on earth. So, it was the interference of the fallen angels – also known as the "watchers" in the book of Enoch – that brought about the violence and corruption of the earth that moved God to bring the flood."

I know I am probably going to get some "correcting" about this from some of the Christians but I have to say that this does make perfect sense, especially considering that one of the things that the "Watchers" gave man was technology, aka knowledge. The ruling elite (the people who actually run the world right now) worship an angel of light because he gives them knowledge....

So what does all of this have to do with gods and goddesses? I believe that these are the gods and goddesses of old. Please bear with me here, I will tie it together soon.

Before I go any further here though, I do want to point out one error that keeps repeating in many of this type of site. Many sites like this want to say that angels or other civilizations were on earth prior to Adam and Eve. This is simply not the case! Science has proven that this is un-likely at best. Creation science (which in my opinion is the real science) shows evidence that the earth is very young. I talk more about this in Evolution and Creation, but I bring it up here because the pre-Adam civilization as some of these groups want to call it draws into question the ownership of the earth! The earth was created *for* man and man *for* the earth. To place another race here before us is to negate our claim on our world!

How important is what we believe??

Many UFO believers/followers, genuinely believe that Genesis 6; follows with the abduction scenario around the world today. Unfortunately, they always want to stop here, just before the Bible starts talking about Gods destruction of earth via worldwide flood, because these events corrupted the earth and humanity so badly! (If you are going to use the Bible as corroboration of your beliefs, use the whole of the information not just what aids your cause).

These are "the gods of old - men of renown" So who exactly are these beings? Do they have names? Sure they do, names like Baal, Isis, Osiris, Hercules, Zeus and Apollo to name a just a few. Do these names sound familiar to you? They should, they are popping up everywhere these days. Paganism, witchcraft and the occult are being cleverly intermingled with evolution, aliens, UFOs and science fiction to give us a fantasy world that is beyond belief! Mix this with dream land type mind control and WOW!

Did you know that there are literally dozens of gods/ goddesses being worshiped in the world right this very minute? What if these beings are real? Do you know what they actually stand for? People want to believe that these beings are benevolent and that somehow by worshiping them they can get what they want, but guess what? God has already shown them to be weak and powerless against him. The only real power that they have is your faith! Which of course, is obtained through means of deceit.

So when was Gods show of power? Have you ever heard of Moses? Did you know that every plague that was brought down on Egypt directly discredited one or more of their gods? I would like to recommend the book "The Gods Who Walk Among Us" By Thomas R Horn and Donald C Jones, PH.D. I am not going to go into a lot of detail here, but I am going to give you a quick rundown of the gods and goddesses that were shown impotent by Gods plagues:

1: The Nile plague; 1) Khnum 2) Sati 3) Hapi 4) Osiris 5) Hathor 6) Neith 7) Sobek and 8) Apepi

2: the Frog plague; Heka

3: the plague of lice; 1) Ra 2) Pharaoh (who was supposedly the incarnation of Horus 3) Geb 4) Seth

4: Plague of flies; Vatchit or Baalzebub, lord of the flies (also known to be a demon)

5: the Deadly murrain; 1) *the Apis Bull, believed to be an incarnation of Osiris 2) Ptah, 3) Hathor and 4) Osiris

6: the Plague of boils; 1) Sekhmet 2) Ptah 3) Osiris 4) Isis

7: the plague of hail; 1) Nut 2) Geb 3) Amun Ra 4) Osiris 5) Pharaoh

8: the plague of locusts; 1) Sobek 2) Ra 3) Shu

9: the plague of darkness; 1) Amun Ra 2) Nut 3) Hathor 4) Isis

10: death of the firstborn; 1) Heka 2) Isis 3) Min 4) Horus 5) Bes

Basically about 2 dozen gods and goddesses were shown worthless against God in just a matter of days! After this God parted the red sea and sent a pillar of fire to guide the Israelites by night and a pillar of smoke by day and yet they *still* were willing to deny God and create a golden calf as their God! Amazing!

The Apis Bull was considered to be the incarnation of God on earth. Basically it was a demonization of the life of Jesus Christ! This is most likely what the Israelites were creating when they made the golden calf. Kind of gives a whole new perspective doesn't it?

Isis is directly related to Crystals and healing magic, when you see crystals in new age shops and other places, this is the goddess being honored!

I would like to take a minute here to mention a particularly interesting god Baal. Baal is actually more of a sur title meaning lord, usually followed by a descriptive name such as ze-bub (of flies) berith (covenant) Gad (fortune) so Baal Gad means lord of fortune. Baalzebub, means lord of the flies. Baal or the equivalent thereof was worshiped by Egyptians, Babylonians, Phoenicians and especially Carthaginians. Now I want to tell you something particularly interesting about the worship of this particular deity.

Baal altars were basically a metal statue with outstretched hands (to hold something) with a metal brazier under his hands in which a fire blazed. What worshipers seeking favor from Baal (usually financial) did was place their living baby in the hands and burn their baby alive as a sacrifice to Baal. This altar was called the place of laughing because as the limbs and muscles contracted the child's open mouth appeared to be laughing! Pretty gruesome, wouldn't you say? Of course there is absolutely no way something like this could happen today right?

Did you know that if you do an on-line search of Wicca or Paganism you will find sites that promote the worship of gods and goddesses, including Baal? One site that I visited actually gave instructions on how to build an altar to Baal! No, they weren't suggesting human sacrifice, at least not yet, but the fact remains that the old gods are making a comeback!

So do you really think that individual beliefs are important? Do you see a pattern?

Now for the science fiction fans, I do apologize, but this correlation is necessary. (Remember that I to, am a sci-fi fan). Star Gate was one of my all time favorites, but I know that this program was absolutely loaded with gods and goddesses, starting with the Egyptian god Ra and continuing through a pantheon of gods and goddesses spanning several cultures. To name just a few: Amaterasu; Japanese sun goddess, Yu, Huang Shang Ti; Chinese god of heaven and earth, Anubis; Egyptian jackal god note the animal reference connected with many Egyptian gods/goddesses, Baal; of course, we have already covered him, Camulus; Celtic god of war, Chalchiuhtlicue; Aztec goddess of water and childbirth, Ishku; Sumarian god of storms, Telchak; Mayan rain god, Marduk; Babylonian, Nirrti; Hindu goddess of death.. Just to name a few and gain a little perspective. I should also mention that there were *benevolent* gods as well, Thor, (Norse god) for example represented by beings that UFO believers call grays, helped SG1 with various problems throughout the history of the show.

However the fact remains that this is a prime example of how gods and goddesses are becoming increasingly well known in our society.

Of course it also creates a connection between aliens and gods/goddesses! It is important to note this.

Of course this is hardly the only example. The truth is that this theme or similar themes are showing up on a very regular basis.

I can't help but wonder how many people watch these highly entertaining shows and movies and never make a connection?! Let's look at a few more examples.

'The Lightening Thief' is loaded with the dark imagery of gods and goddesses.

'Avatar', was absolutely gorgeous! Once again however loaded with goddess imagery, not to mention some "alien" reference, and of course we have the evil un-accepting humans, bent on destroying the world of these beings for greed. I want to examine a little closer just what is being presented here. First, you have the very tall (9-12 ft?) cat like beings, who just happens to be blue. Then we have the (benevolent) goddess Eywa (Gaia reference) of this world who is connected with everything on the planet, plants people and even the souls of the dead. This goddess or connection has the ability to transfer a soul from one body to another. And, leave us not forget the evil humans who simply want to destroy the world with no respect for this world, race or their beliefs.

OK, first, we have the very tall cat-like people this covers both the Nephilim (giants) and the half human, half animal aspect of Egyptian gods/goddesses. They are blue, this covers not only the Hindu goddess Krishna but some of the gods and goddesses of other cultures are blue as well. The Hopi religion speaks of blue gods that they call Kachinas. Then you have the goddess who actually interacts with the plants and inhabitants of this world, (Pandora, is the name of this world, no mythology references here!). Then we have the plant/goddess ability to transfer a soul from one being to another. I read somewhere once (don't quote me, I don't remember many of the details) that the so-called *aliens* who abduct people have the ability to do this as well. I seem to recall an incident where the soul of a man was transferred into the body of a woman because he was more comfortable in a female body. I would also mention here that abductees' sometimes refer to a smell of sulfur attached to some of these beings. Just an interesting little observation, since another word for sulfur, is brimstone, I just think this is noteworthy...LOL.

Last but not least, the evil uncaring humans who show no respect for these beings or their world. This is of course a reference to the evil Christians who do not accept the worship of other gods or goddesses. I know that Christians were not mentioned specifically in the movie, but the intolerance was. In all fairness though since this took place on another world Humans really wouldn't have a claim, but making humanity look selfish and intolerant (one statement in the movie was that the humans had killed their goddess) was definitely on the agenda here! Actually this is backwards, average man is being made to believe that he is destroying mother earth, but it is followers of the Angel of light or Satan that are in fact destroying the earth. Before I get away from this subject I would like to mention that I ran an on-line search for the goddess Eywa of Avatar and yielded some very interesting results. Did you know that thousands of people reported being depressed, even suicidal after watching Avatar? They comment that the world of Pandora was so vivid and real that the average mundane world seems dull after watching this movie! No seduction into goddess worship here!!!

Another comment from watchers of Avatar was that they want to be one of the Na'vi (one of the cat-like residents of Pandora). Hmm. Please check out the article at www.cross.to/articles2/010/avatar.htm this article begins with the statement Blending Hinduism, Shamanism and God Spirituality. (Hmm seem to have forgotten about the Egyptian animal/human hybrid message)

A few more things that I would like to touch on before I move on. The word AVATAR refers to an incarnation or manifestation of a Hindu God! Most common are incarnations of Visnu, Krishna and Rama. One reviewer commented: "A film with some REAL religion in it! Another comment that I found interesting was: that Eywa sounds like Yahweh backwards! And it does! I do believe that this is an interesting tell all by itself!

The one most important aspect of all of this is that this movie (amongst others) seems to want to imply that man (aside from an enlightened few) is inherently evil this is not true! Two things that I want to touch on here. One, Man was not created evil, evil or sin was in fact introduced to us by the very being(s) who introduced man to sin in the first place! Man may not have been created evil but he sure does seem to be easily influenced and easily seduced into new, seemingly beneficial, ways of thinking! We can convince ourselves that something is right if it seems to benefit us in some way! Second, implying that man is inherently evil and getting people to believe this makes it appear perfectly reasonable to annihilate most of us, perhaps in favor of another race such as a human hybrid of say, an alien, or god/goddess, fallen angel!? Of course the remaining population should be servants or slaves to this new race. This is of course the ultimate goal and that is where the real deception lies!

Unfortunately, the thing that people do not see or understand (largely due to thought control efforts) is that this beautiful out of this world existence that they are looking for isn't in these deceptive places, it is in GOD. Man was created in God image! God is a *creator*! This means that we are also creative beings!

Just think about this, if man can create such a fantastic beautiful world in the fantasy of movies, just think what we as co-inheritors with Jesus Christ can create when sin and evil no longer exist!

With the re-emergence of gods and goddesses in *Christian* society though, it is important that we notice how these types of beings are being integrated into society and how anyone who takes a stand against this process is portrayed as evil!

Oh, I know that this has been a *gradual* shift in our perception of the world at large, but the shift is there none the less! The truth is that many people these days (including some *Christians*) are opening the door to different types of religion!

The thing that I want to point out here is this: Exodus 20:4 "Thou shall have no other gods before me." This is the number one commandment!!!! This could not be any clearer! I would also like to point out here that throughout history, it has never ended well for the people who worshiped other gods! Especially God's people!

How important is what we believe?

A good question here is: how many examples of gods, goddesses, aliens, UFOs, mythical creatures (many of whom are associated with paganism and the occult) and outright idolatry do you have in your home, at work, on your computer or on your person right this very moment? I would bet that if you really took a good hard look, that you would be very surprised!

Do you read your horoscope? This is an occult practice related to star worship! Do you have pictures or other images of fairies, gnomes, ogres, leprechauns or elves in your home or elsewhere? Again these are directly associated with occult practices and beliefs!

Do you carry a talisman or good luck charm? These are often associated with some type of idolatry! Do the research, you will be surprised! A few weeks ago, my husband received a letter in the mail which wanted to sell him this "good luck" amulet. On the amulet were the letters Re. Having just recently done a lot of research on gods and goddesses I recognized the name immediately. I said R E, this is another spelling for the Egyptian god Ra! He then read a little further and they explained that they did discover that this symbol was Egyptian in origin, but nowhere in the letter did they make the connection that this was a symbol of the Egyptian sun god Ra! Needless to say the letter went into the trash!

How many things like this do you have in your possession? After all these things are lucky, right? They are going to bring us what we want or need the most, right? We are simply told that these are "good luck" talismans of some sort, maybe representing money, health or love and we just accept these things without question. After all what harm can possible come from a good luck charm? Right? Let me ask you this: do these good luck charms actually work?

Oh, I know that many claims are made, especially on the chain letter type that you get through you e-mail, but do you actually receive the promised good luck or fortune?

Anyone who has friends on-line from whom they get e-mail will be familiar with this one: Good luck angels, (yes angel worship is a sin) or good luck Buddha's or any other such portrayal of an entity associated with "*luck*".

When you get these and forward them on to receive your *good luck* or *fortune* you are not only participating in a form of idolatry but you are asking your friends to do the same! Stop and think about this for a moment!

Does this really matter? After all it's all just harmless fun right? Is it? It seems like such a small insignificant thing, but when you add it to the many other ways that paganism, the occult and idolatry are entering your life, it becomes a little bit more serious! Especially, when you stop and consider how God is being removed and demonized!

The real question here is this: How serious do you think that God takes this? Folks whether you realize it or not, this is idolatry! Believe me, God takes this *VERY* seriously!

Exodus 20:4 Thou shalt not make unto thee any graven image, or any likeness *of anything* that *is* in heaven above, or that *is* in the earth beneath, or that *is* in the water under the earth:

Considering that this is one of the original 10 commandments and very near the top, I would say that this is pretty important to God! Wouldn't you agree that this is a logical assumption? Can we really afford to just assume that this is just harmless fun if God himself doesn't think so?

This is just another means by which your thoughts... your beliefs are being altered. Another means by which you are being programmed or told what to think and believe and once again it is another assault on God and the Bible! It is a subtle, seemingly insignificant affront to God, but it is an affront all the same! Of course this is the point!

How important is what we believe?

Folks, please stop and think, how harmless are these things, what beliefs are you passing on to others around you? Please, look at what is going on in the world and at your core beliefs! Do you really want for yourself, your loved ones or your *CHILDREN* (and believe me they are the primary target) to lose their eternal inheritance, their eternal happiness, to a LIE? Whether you want to believe it or not that is what this is...a LIE!

For your sake and the sake of your loved ones, please, consider this. There has been an ongoing attack to remove God and Christianity from our lives. The attacks are generally a reference to Christians being intolerant, judgmental, haters of people who don't believe what they do and of course haters of fun. Of course it's all a lie and completely opposite of the truth!

Christians are about love, not hate. Christians are about joy and happiness.. And eternal salvation! Christians are about TRUTH. Christians are sinners just like everyone else, why would we judge you (yes I suppose there are some who do, but they are generally the exception not the rule)? And FUN, as hard as this might be to understand, drinking, drugs illicit sexual exploits, witchcraft and all of the other worldly things are the things of darkness and emptiness. There is no true joy in these things! When you become one with the creator of the universe is when you begin to realize what true fun and joy really are!

I just want people to realize that being a Christian is a lot different than we imagine it to be, the pure peace and joy are unlike anything that you can imagine!

OH, and yes, I do realize that I sound like an alarmist, after all is anyone really worshiping gods and goddesses here in evolutionary America? You just might be surprised! After all, the door is wide open and has been for some time, and don't forget that 'those who do not remember history are doomed to repeat it'

For example, have you ever heard of Wicca, Paganism, Buddhism, Hinduism, what about Witchcraft or Satanism? All of these things are present here in the USA and many of them have been in practice here for many years! I remember there being a satanic group worshiping near where I grew up back in the 60s and 70s! I also remember hearing that the waiting list for this group was enormous something like 500 and that was 40+ years ago! Just imagine how far we have come since then! Of course, movies like Harry Potter have done much to further the cause, just ask a practicing witch, they will tell you!

Believe me I do realize that this all just seems like a trend and seems harmless enough on the outside, but is it really? Hopefully when you add this up against the bigger picture you will begin to see just how *harmless* this *isn't*!

So, just as an interesting experiment let me give you the names of some gods and goddesses and see how many you recognize. Aphrodite, Apollo, Artemis, Athena, Atlas, Baal, Ceres, Demeter, Dians, Dionysus, El, Enki, Gaia, Hades, Hathor, Hera, Hermes, Horus, Isis, Ishtar, Jupiter, Krishna, Loki, Luna, Mars, Mercury, Minerva, Neptune, the 9 muses, Odin, Osiris, Pan, Phoebe, Poseidon, Quetzacoatl, Ra/Re, Shiva, Thor, Venus, Vishnu and Zeus.

These are the gods/goddesses that I recognized from a list 195 deities that I found on the internet and I know that there are more! Yes, but none of them are actually being worshiped, right? Let me suggest a site for you;

http://paganwiccan.about.com/od/holidaysandcelebrations /u/Celebrations.htm I know it's a long address but a quick search for paganism or even gods and goddesses will also bring you some very interesting results! If you really want to know the truth about god and goddess worship today, just go look! Remember I told you from the beginning of this book that you should do your own research!

How important is what we believe?

I know that for the most part, people tend to believe that all of these movies, TV programs, cartoons and evolutionary teachings are harmless, but are they? I grew up having been taught that evolution actually happened and I know for a fact that this changed my perception of Biblical teachings! Science fiction and fantasy added to my perceptions of the world. This was approximately 50 years ago, how much farther have we come since then?

Now any kid who reads the popular "Magic" books has an instant initiation into paganism! Of course magic books aren't the only source of pagan or deity beliefs, these days you can find gods, goddesses, UFOs, aliens and/or evolutionary Atheism just about everywhere! Especially if you have access to the internet!

Have you noticed the subtle shift from UFOs and aliens to gods and goddesses lately? Yet nearly all if not all abductees or contactee's as they call themselves, are deeply involved in the occult, aka paganism, witchcraft, god/goddess worship and the new age or one world religion.

These people definitely make a connection between these things, yet we are to believe that this is harmless?

AND all the while, we are being told to believe that God has no place, or that Christians are either evil or fools or even that Jesus Christ never actually existed or any number of anti Christian story spins designed specifically to influence your beliefs and draw you away from God!

WHY? I suggest that you read your Bible! It's all there! To deceive if possible even the elect!

Jesus Christ is freedom, salvation, joy, hope and most of all truth! The Bible tells about what is happening and what is still coming, all of this is part of the plan!

You still have your God given free will, for the moment, but the choice is yours, no one else's! You might believe that you are following some wonderful new faith through which "everyone is one with god", maybe you do not believe in any god, or maybe you think that the teachings of magic and goddess worship might be fun, but all of these things lead to one place, you will worship Satan in the end! That is the whole point of all of this! This is the ultimate goal! The New World Order or one world government is well under way, so is the one world religion! Shoot, even Oprah is pushing that agenda as well as our beloved President! AND, whether you like it or not, whether you choose to believe it or not, this is exactly what the Bible said would and will happen!

So why do you *REALLY* think that they are trying to destroy Christianity? Can't have people around who know the truth, now can we? Remember, the ultimate goal is the destruction and or enslavement of the human race! Why? Jealousy mostly! Man was created in God's image, to be a family to God, and Satan hates us for this, He believes that he (or they, fallen angels) is superior to us and that we are usurpers of his birthright, and he hates us. He wants us to worship him, not God, thereby guaranteeing our destruction and giving him revenge!

I realize that there are a lot of people who will look at this statement and call it superstitious nonsense, but take a good hard look at what is really happening in the world, do the research and try to see beyond the surface appearance of what you see and hear. If you look close enough, you will see a pattern and if you compare it to the Bible, you will see a lot more!

This much I am certain about...time is running out!

If you do not take control of your thoughts, someone else will!

Some links to get you started on your search for the truth!

http://www.stevequayle.com/Giants/pics/giants.html

http://www.youtube.com/watch?v=T4jdrPG0C94&feature
=related

http://www.youtube.com/watch?v=D5aOP-azKzs&feature
=related

A quick note here, some of these links may not be working. Links that contain *"uncomfortable"* information for certain groups have a tendency to disappear or attacks are launched to make the information appear false.

Aliens and Angels

Are you being told what to think?

It has been estimated that approximately 80% of Americans believe in UFOs and this number may even be higher in some other countries, Mexico for example is currently known to be a UFO hot spot.

Do I believe in the existence of UFOs and Aliens? OR even the possibility of alien abductions? Yes, I do. I just do not believe that these beings are what they are being presented to be. I believe that the words fallen angels or demons are far more likely! I do believe that these beings have been here on, in or above the earth nearly as long as we have.

There are many references in the Bible to fallen angels, giants and the Nephilim as well as some pretty interesting descriptions of other beings, such as the beings described in Ezekiel 1.

However, the Bible isn't the only place where interesting beings appear! Nearly every civilization on earth has references to some type of god or gods that allegedly provided them with knowledge or technology.

A quick note here; we (our generation) has a tendency to believe that we are *better* or more *evolved* than our ancestors, We assume that since we have more technology that we are somehow more advanced, but is this true? What if I told you that we are not evolving, we are in fact devolving?! We are (see evolution vs. creation). Remember we do not possess the technology today to build the pyramids, nor do we have surgical scalpels that are anywhere near as sharp (even today) as the obsidian scalpels that the Mayans had 2000 years ago!

I just wanted to point out that we do not know as much as we like to think that we do.

Anyway, many of the ancient cultures have stories of visitors or gods who appeared and allegedly gave them technologies and knowledge that advanced their civilizations. Interestingly enough, many of these civilizations also engaged in human sacrifice on a regular basis. Have you ever considered that there might be a connection?

The Illuminati (yes they are real) worship an angel of light. Yes, they do know that this is Satan. They despise God because he 'withholds' information from man, while Satan is made the hero because he gives man knowledge and technology. This group of people thinks of us average people as sheep to be ruled over and have no qualms what so ever about sacrificing any of us to advance their plans or to get what they want. Do you think this is just a coincidence? Do the research.

Now anybody who has done any kind of UFO/alien research will be familiar with the abduction scenario. Back in the 90s, 50% of the population believed that people have been abducted, with 3% believing that they had been abducted, which may not sound like many but actually is about 800,000 people (and this was in the 90's).

The story goes (and this is pretty common) that people are *taken* by small gray beings usually during the night, but sometimes from other places as well. These beings always know where their "subjects" are and there appears to be some kind of mind/thought control in action here that seems to sedate not only the abductees, but everyone else who might be around as well. They are taken aboard some type of craft and experimented on. These people have implants put in them in various parts of their bodies. Often women are impregnated, only to have the pregnancy terminated after a few months. Sexual experiments are done on men also *there are reports of men being forced to impregnate alien females*, often a few years later these people are introduced to their hybrid children. All of these abductees report some kind of "teaching" that takes place, supposedly in some kind of effort to save the planet, etc. I would like to point out the marked similarity of visitations of bygone years by Incubus and Succubus entities. Think about it, isn't this what these beings did, commit perverse sexual acts or rape acts upon humans?

Many such abductees' say that they hate these experiences and their abductors while others seem to have some kind of *relationship* with these beings.

One thing that is always present in these visits or abductions is an altered state of consciousness. This altered state of mind also seems to transfer to people around them as well. This might explain why people around them never seem to remember these events. Whether these are actually abductions or some type of guided hallucination is a subject of some debate, however without an actual physical visit of some sort pregnancies are problematical.

I tend to want to believe that these are inter-dimensional beings that can physically appear in our dimension. This seems logical to me because of the unusual abilities that the craft seem to possess, such as impossible right angle turns at very high speeds, or simply vanishing.

In the book UFOs in the New Age, author William M Alnor also believes these being to be from another dimension and makes some very interesting parallels to the other worldly beings which the UFO cults are trying to inject into society as space brothers and *saviors,* with the known evil entities from the past! I highly recommend this book, it is currently out of print but I found it very easily on www.amazon. com. Mr. Alnors research is extensive and to be honest after reading his book I had to reevaluate some of my own conclusions! I do have to say that it is interesting how so very many different people can reach the same conclusion about this phenomenon without ever having spoken with each other or had any other contact with their ideas or research. I do believe that God is talking through some of us to deliver this message to the world and showing us what he wants us to know. I asked God for the truth many years ago, He has given me this truth but I also believe that with truth comes the responsibility of that truth, which is of course why I am writing this book. Mr. Alnor made a similar statement near the end of his book, an urgent message from God? It seems that for all of us trying to get this message through to people, where one leaves off another picks up, this is fascinating to me and fills me with a profound sense of wonder and awe! Thank you lord!

As I said earlier I also believe that these beings are evil. This definitely falls under the classification of end-times delusion! I also believe that the more research that you do yourself the better, of course you have to want to know the truth, and unfortunately many people seem to prefer the lie of space brotherhood or a new exciting religion to the truth, but know this; the Bible has been researched by many, many scholars throughout the centuries and has been proven true, it continues to be proven true and accurate through science today (though you have to seek this information). If you want the truth, do the research!

Possibly the biggest part of this deception is the fact that people seem to believe that they have no control and that these *beings* have all of the power. This is a lie.

Unfortunately, if they can get you to believe it then it's true! What I mean by this is that if you *believe* that they can just take you, then they can! It's called free will! These beings have been around nearly as long as man himself, don't you think that they know this? So why is it, human beings do not know this?

To begin with, the book which contains this truth has been made to appear antiquated and false, beginning with the attack on the Bible using the theory of evolution. It has of course continued on over the years with a pantheon of new attacks, new age doctrines of many types (including some very old god/goddess/idolatry practices), the message that God doesn't belong in schools and public places, and of course the introduction of paganism or witchcraft practices in the place where children are most vulnerable...<u>school</u>*!*

'Think about this; Children are being indoctrinated into these beliefs and the one book that provides them with the protection of truth is not allowed! Think this is just a coincidence?

How important is what we believe?

UFO's and aliens are nothing more than a new spin on an old story. AND despite the beliefs of abductees that these creatures are somehow benevolent (here to help us, a theme that is sometimes repeated in movies and TV programs) they are not! They do have an agenda and it certainly has nothing to do with helping humanity!

These beings are known to kidnap, rape, mutilate and murder! Does this really sound like they have mans best interest in mind? Nearly everyone has heard of the famous Roswell crash of 1947. The army captures a crashed UFO and recovers a live 'Grey' alien is reported one day and the next day the report is 'oh it was just a weather balloon'. Like army personnel would not know the difference...! This is not the only crash site for UFOs, there have been other crash sites in various places around the world. I have to say that this has always seemed suspect to me. I mean, these beings have been around for thousands of years and now suddenly they are crashing their ships which nearly always results in wreckage and debris being collected along with bodies and even live *aliens*! It's just a little too convenient if you ask me, and this just happens to be taking place right around the time that we are testing our new A bomb and around the time that Evolution is making its way into public venues like schools. (A quick note; 1947, also happens to be the year that famous Satanist; Aleister Crowley died!). For those of you who are unfamiliar with this, Mr. Crowley once claimed to have made contact with a alternate dimensional being who bore a strong resemblance to the small gray aliens who most people are familiar with today. Hmm.

It just sounds a little too much like the Garden of Eden to me in the respect that man is being offered a little taste of the knowledge that *could* be available to him. You have to admit that we have made some pretty amazing strides in the last 60 years!

For the most part, it is generally believed now that the US government did try to cover this up, for a couple of reasons first would be a security issue. Can't have people thinking that their government can't protect them, and of course the acquisition of new technology, we certainly do not want to share any of this!

The security issue really comes into play in 1952 when on 3 consecutive weekend's clusters of low flying UFO's buzzed Washington DC. This was picked up on both civilian and military radar, and was reported in newspapers. During these events the intelligence communications channels became so clogged up with reports of UFO's that had a foreign power chosen that time to attack no messages could have gotten through to the pentagon! I'm sure this must have made an interesting impression on the US Government, but again, it seems a little too *planned* to me. After all fear can be a pretty powerful motivator!

Interestingly enough, 1952 is also the year that the USA began their mind control program known as MGM Ultra or MK Ultra. This began with a study done by the CIA on how the average human would react when faced by an enemy.

There is a rumor (Nobody seems to know if this is true or not but it does fit) that Eisenhower met with aliens in the spring of 1954 and reached an agreement by which the Grey's (small gray skinned aliens with big eyes) would provide the US with space technology and in return would be allowed to carry out genetic experiments on humans (aka US Citizens). I have read accounts that the *Greys* were not the only race of beings to have contacted the US government and also that the agreement has since been broken by them. I tend to want to be leery of this because it gets into realms I would rather avoid.

However from the stand point of cover up and debunking it does make a lot of sense. The US government began a policy back in 1947 of debunking and covering up, any and all UFO reports. This began officially in 1947 with project blue book which supposedly ended in 1969 however reports were still going on in the 1990s.

Information released via the freedom of information act always have large sections of text 'blacked out' supposedly for reasons of national security, text released in the 90s are far more heavily blacked out than pages from the 60s 70s and 80s! Of course the 1990s was a time of heavy UFO activity all over the world as well as in this country. The thing that is most interesting about this is that, the US govt. is still denying these. Although, there seems to be a shift in policy though since programs such as; "Confirmation, Hard Evidence of Aliens among Us" began appearing on the major TV stations in the 90s. All of the major information Media has been owned by the ruling elite for several decades, so the fact that this information has made its way to main stream TV is interesting. However this still allows for the distrust of the US government by her citizens and this is (by my opinion) deliberate. (more on this later in this book)

The thing that you need to keep in mind here is that there are many, many major scientists, doctors and researchers who take this *very* seriously, they believe that this needs to be studied and taken seriously by the government as well as civilian facilities. I can't help but wonder why the US government would be one of the few who still deny the existence of UFOs?

The most rational explanation to me is that to release information to the people of the USA (or the people of the world for that matter) is to release information of just how deep their own involvement goes. In other words they do not want the US people to know what their own government has been doing to them, or has allowed to be done to them, and the main reason for this is greed. It is no secret that the US government has always gone after the most advanced technology and will take any measures necessary to get it! To be fair, I suppose that if the USA wants to remain the last superpower that it is important to have the most current technology, I just take issue with the *means* of doing so as well as the alternate uses for the technology!

An interesting little side note here: In a UFO related search I discovered a link for a site called "The God Who Wasn't There" Disputing the existence of Jesus Christ! You can look yourself at www.thegodmovie.com I find this an interesting correlation, don't you?

So who or what are these so called *aliens*? One site that I visited reports around 30 different 'species' of alien believed to be alive and well and living on planet earth!

Perhaps the most well know of these would be the Greys. This is the one that people generally associate with abductions or visitations. One of these that I find particularly interesting is the blues. What I find particularly interesting about this species is the fact that many blue gods and goddesses appear in various religions throughout the world. Do you think that there might be a connection? Do you think that there could be a connection in Avatar? How about this, the blue skinned Andoreans in Star Trek? Interesting!

Something that I would like to mention here is that whether these beings are real or not isn't as important as what we *believe* about them!

How important is what we believe?

There are people who are trying to convince abductees' that this is a form of waking dream or night terror experience, but it doesn't quite sound convincing. This is however a possibility or maybe even was true in the beginning, either way, the one thing that nobody seems to want to touch on is the fact that all of these experiences are extremely similar! So, if this actually were an experience of the mind, then it was a *controlled* experience! This *is* quite possible! It is possible that these nightmare images are or were planted as a mind control experiment. My research suggests that this is likely a very real scenario, however even if this were a mind control experiment it is/was likely a preview of actual coming events, since this fit's in far too well with scripture.

Luke17:24 – 26 For as the lightening, that lighteneth out of the one part under heaven, shineth unto the other part under heaven; so shall also the Son of man be in his day 25; But first he must suffer many things, and be rejected of this generation 26; And <u>as it was in the days of Noah, so shall it also be in the days of the son of man.</u>

Yes, I know I am omitting passages, but this does fit the current scenario, especially when you stop and consider that Jesus Christ is pretty much being rejected by the country that embraced Christ as their foundation. There are a growing number of people these days that believe that the coupling of Angels with Humans was an effort by Satan to pollute Human DNA and prevent the Birth of Jesus Christ. If indeed there was an effort by Satan and his followers to corrupt mans DNA and thereby destroy him (and prevent the birth of Jesus Christ) then it is quite possible that with the ongoing effort to remove Jesus from the minds of men that Satan and his followers would indeed try every means available to destroy man again, before man can reclaim his inheritance! [A quick search of aliens UFOs should give you more information on this].This could easily include the creation of gods and goddesses or super powerful hybrids, (same scenario different names). This would also encompass nearly every belief system on the planet from Atheist (either evolution or aliens created us) to Paganism (gods and goddesses). Everything except those darned intolerant Christians and Jews who believe that these are evil beliefs! It all leads to the same place though, the worship of false gods and idols!

So once again, how important is what we believe?

Doesn't it seem to you that everyone with any kind of power or control in this world is pulling out all of the stops in an all out effort to gain control of your beliefs? You might want to keep in mind that what you believe is directly connected with your free will! Think about this!

So how harmful are those sci-fi movies and TV shows?

Harry Potter, books are good because they get kids to read, aren't they? Avatar was beautiful, how could this be a bad thing? Do the people watching these things have any familiarity with Biblical history? Are people aware that these things lead down a road to destruction? Do people even realize that they are being *TOLD* what to believe? Do people understand that they are being indoctrinated into a belief that requires acceptance of other worldly beings and that not accepting them makes you an evil intolerant being, worthy of being destroyed?

People when you are watching these programs really pay attention to the general theme of this programming. Watch for the innuendo's and pay attention to how the program directs your thoughts and emotions, I can pretty much promise you that anyone who doesn't accept the alien/god/goddess is portrayed as evil and needs to be stopped and or destroyed!

Of course there is always the other scenario, which bears mention here as well, in which the aliens are evil and bent on mans destruction, (scare tactics) in which case God is never even mentioned, which implies that God is uncaring or impotent, or simply just doesn't exist and we are on our own! (The 'we don't want to be alone' theme seems to be pretty common among UFO believers) Either way Christians are portrayed as either evil or idiots! Pay attention folks, this *IS* the message here! AND it *IS* planned this way!

I mentioned earlier that UFO sightings are increasing throughout the world. There are always lots of eyewitness reports, often very credible, such as police officers, who witness huge objects that have the ability to temporarily stop car functions, move at incredible speeds and make impossible high speed turns.

Now I am going to make an observation that no one else seems to have made.

I can't help but think that this is basically a dog and pony show. It seems to me that all of these sightings are designed to be a show of power and advanced technology, the purpose of which is to make us believe that we are somehow inferior to them! If this were true, then why is there a need to control our thoughts and beliefs? Why the need for darkness? Why the need to eliminate Christianity? Make no mistake this is part of their agenda! Is it because Christians are evil intolerant people? We are certainly being told that this is true! In his book UFO's in the New Age, William Alnor draws the same conclusion, in fact his research shows this as the central theme of entering into a relationship with the so called aliens/angels. Abductees' are usually drawn into some form of channeling and or spiritism and there is always a repeating theme of trying to destroy God, the word of god (the Bible) and or Jesus Christ himself! These range from 'Jesus Christ never really existed' to 'Jesus was an alien and doesn't want to be worshiped'! However the story goes it is always about destroying Christianity! An interesting note here; many of the contactee's in this book are lied to repeatedly by these beings, yet they feel that these beings are good and ultimately have our best interests at heart!

Remember that I said earlier that you cannot be taken or abducted if you know that you can't? This is something that God made me aware of many years ago and since then I have found inter-net sites and other accounts of people who have discovered this fact for themselves!

The simple fact of the matter is that if you belong to God these beings cannot take you unless you give them permission to do so! They cannot violate your God given free will! AND this fact carries throughout everything that I am talking about in this book! You have to give them permission to take you or do anything to you!

I know that there are people who will look at this statement and say that I am crazy, but I know for a fact that this is true! However, if they can make you *BELIEVE* that they can take you or assault you against your will, then guess what...they can!

It boils down to this; if you *believe* that they are stronger than you, they are! If you *believe* that they are far more advanced and powerful, then they are! AND unfortunately these are supernatural beings who know every fear and weakness that you have, and how to use this knowledge against you!

On the other hand if you *know* that they cannot take you against your will, then they can't! If you *know* or *believe* that God gives us power and authority then you have power and authority!

Our shelter and strength is in Jesus Christ and our faith and trust in him! The closer that you are to Christ, the stronger you are and the fewer ways the enemy has to get to you! That is not to say that he won't keep trying, he will, even through the people you love, but Christ is your protection and salvation, your assurance of your inheritance and the evil ones know this!

Why else do you think that all of these different things are so focused on eliminating Christianity? They know full well that if you do not have access to Jesus Christ that you are vulnerable! If you are vulnerable then you can be controlled! To control what you believe is to control free will! You have to want to be a slave!

On a program called "Confirmation – Hard Evidence of Aliens Among Us" there is a statement from a woman who calls herself a 'starling' her name is Ann Rajaiuoma, who claims to be a hybrid reborn on earth, who's family is supposedly on the planet Sirius. She claims that her mission here is to "let people know about cosmic things and life in the universe that is a mystery to man." She also claims to be from the 3rd *hierarchy of angels.*

Now aside from her unusually long fingers she looks normal enough, maybe she should be locked up in a mental institution? Except for the one thing that kind of got my attention... "to let people know" *knowledge*! Isn't this what the fallen angels offer man repeatedly throughout history? Isn't this the one thing that always leads us down the path of sin that ends in destruction?

This statement alone makes me wonder if she could be telling the truth?!

If there really is an effort under way to create a hybrid race, then this is the ultimate goal, the destruction of man!

I am uncertain as to just how much information to give you. Some of the information is pretty grizzly and pretty frightening and it is certainly not my intention to scare the wits out of people, in fact the point of this book is just the opposite, to make people realize that there is hope and that they do not need to live in fear! To live in fear is to give others control over you!

Last night (March 6, 2010) I watched a program on the History channel named *Ancient Aliens*. Which was basically a rundown of Erich Von Daniken's 'Chariots of the Gods', theories about the appearance of other worldly beings throughout the history of the world, as portrayed in religious artifacts, architecture, art and writings. (Please keep in mind that this was on the *HISTORY* channel! Which tends to give things that have no real scientific merit, such as evolution, a respectable scientific appearance, this is important!)

In May 2008 the Vatican made a startling proclamation that "life might exist on other planets and a belief in extraterrestrials did not contradict a belief in God"

Interesting, wouldn't you say?

Another *Spiritual* person being interviewed on this program is a Rev. Barry H Downing. Author of '*The Bible and flying saucers*'

Who states; "We are entering an age where the universe is conceived of in different ways, replacing angels of 2000 years ago with high tech angels of now. We have this *inner need to feel that were not alone in the universe*. We're scientific people and we'd be embarrassed to call them angels because we stopped believing in that kind of *superstitious stuff* but we still believe in aliens from another planet" (Do you see a message here?)

Please keep in mind that these are supposedly religious people! Erich Von Daniken claims to believe in God, he has clearly read the Bible, yet he is either missing the big picture or is disregarding the warning for the sake of his bottom line!

I am trying very hard not to appear as a crazed religious zealot here, although I am not sure I am succeeding at this, just let me say that I am NOT this kind of person. What I AM is someone who sees a pattern here that has me deeply concerned. I hope that you will see it too by the end of this book.

There are 2 assumptions in this program that I want to address here. 1) It is assumed that we are smarter and more evolved than our ancestors that they were not mentally capable of comprehending what they were seeing! 2) Most of their beliefs about this center around evolution! Which means; that their assumptions are flawed from the very beginning! Anyone who actually looks at the science of creation, actually *looks* at it, will realize pretty quickly that the evidence supports creation (the Biblical account of creation) not evolution! AND if creation is true, then you really need to reevaluate your facts! Also the assumption that we are more evolved and intelligent than our ancestors would be a really big mistake to make if creation is true, because by the creation model we are not evolving, we are devolving! The fact that we keep developing new genetic diseases and shorter life spans would seem to testify to this fact all by itself! Yet, we are so self absorbed and arrogant that we refuse to see past our own fleeting achievements! Amazing!

Von Daniken makes a couple of statements that I would like to mention here, He is talking about how he started studying different religions of every mythology and " the story is always the same-of course with different names. Somebody descends, Our forefathers couldn't understand it, they believed that these are some gods." "nearly every religion has similar stories of deities with spectacular powers and abilities who come to earth and directly influence the lives of men. The so-called gods are here, they give orders, they *force* the humans to do certain things, then they disappear with the promise that they will appear in the far away future."

{Interestingly, Jesus Christ is pictured here as well! This is an important little fact! It shows the thinking and the message!}

The thing that always seems to get left out of these accounts is the fact that (not including Jesus Christ of course) most of these religions practiced human sacrifice! Nor did these religions seem to benefit their people in any way that makes them anything but a servant or a slave! Does this fact really seem like a coincidence to you?

Many accounts of these gods are of giant gods who are extremely cruel to humans and often devour them! Are these really the beings that we want here on earth? Yet many people seem to want just that! WHY? Probably because they do not know the whole story! There is a profound danger in not looking at all of the available information! [Do they really believe that since we are now more technologically advanced that we are somehow to be considered equal by these beings?] Yet over and over again this is the story, just use the information that suits our purpose and omit the part that we do not like!

This program talks about the various pyramids around the world, the great pyramid at Giza was said to have been built in 22 years. This program claims that this is impossible, man would have to cut, move and place one block every 9 seconds. OK, has anyone ever heard of the coral castle?

You can find the story at: http://paranormal.about.com/od/moremadscience/a/coral-castle-secrets.htm this excerpt is taken from this site,

Coral Castle in Homestead, Florida, is one of the most amazing structures ever built. In terms of accomplishment, it's been compared to Stonehenge, ancient Greek temples, and even the great pyramids of Egypt. It is amazing - some even say miraculous - because it was quarried, fashioned, transported, and constructed by one man: Edward Leedskalnin, a 5-ft. tall, 100-lb. Latvian immigrant.

Many men have single-handedly built their own homes, but Leedskalnin's choice of building materials is what makes his undertaking so incredible. He used huge blocks of coral rock, some weighing as much as 30 tons, and somehow was able to move them and set them in place without assistance or the use of modern machinery. And therein lies the mystery. How did he do it?

It's estimated that 1,000 tons of coral rock were used in construction of the walls and towers, and an additional 100 tons of it were carved into furniture and art objects:

When he was personally asked how he managed the feat, Leedskalnin replied only that he understood the laws of weight and leverage. He is quoted as saying, "I have discovered the secrets of the pyramids. I have found out how the Egyptians and the ancient builders in Peru, Yucatan, and Asia, with only primitive tools, raised and set in place blocks of stone weighing many tons."

According to The Enigma of Coral Castle, "Ed flatly disagreed with modern science, and claimed that the scientists were wrong, 'that nature is simple.' He believed all matter consisted of individual magnets, and it is the movement of these magnets within materials, and through space, that produce measurable phenomena, magnetism, and electricity. These concepts 'involved the relationship of the Earth to celestial alignments.' He claimed to see beads of light which he believed to be the physical presence of nature's magnetism and life force, or what we term today, chi."

Impossible! Really? I will also mention here that he moved his entire castle in one night!

I am sure that you have probably heard of George Noory, talk show host of the unusual and paranormal. He too was featured on this program in support of the ancient astronaut theory. He made this statement: "You mean to tell me that people of that time period did this by hand? I don't think so!" Again, this is such an arrogant statement!

We assume that since we can't figure out how to do something that our ancient forefathers couldn't either! Keep in mind that this people was closer to creation, so their brains more than likely functioned much clearer and better than our polluted brains! Just because we think something is impossible, it doesn't make it so!

I would also like to point out that the world wide flood story exists in most parts of the world as well, throughout many religious cultures! AND the math confirms that the world's population from the flood of Noah until now at a growth rate of 2.5 would give us a world population of 6.5 billion people, the current world population! And every human being on earth can trace his/her ancestry to 1 of 4 men. Noah and his 3 sons! This means that we are all related. So if we are all related then why is it so difficult to think that we can build similar structures all over the world?

Of course the argument could easily be made that the *sons of God,* taking wives of the *daughters of men* and creating unnatural offspring (Nephilim) and otherwise corrupting humanity with forbidden knowledge, was the cause of the flood in the first place! (I am playing devil's advocate here, looking at both sides)

And yes, it is possible, that beings from another world, aka *fallen* angels may have shown this knowledge to men (possible) but considering that these *gods* thought of man as servants or slaves it is unlikely that they actually did any of the physical labor!

However none of this in any way indicates that our ancestors were, in any way, less intelligent than we are today! I would like to repeat a famous quote; "those who do not remember history are doomed to repeat it"! I do genuinely believe that there are people in this world who are counting on this fact! AND many of them are actually pushing this agenda!

So, how important is what we believe?

It is interesting that all of these religions/mythologies claim that these beings came from the sky, especially when you stop and consider that Satan is known as the lord of the sky!

Von Daniken likes to make the statement that his God is almighty and wouldn't need vehicles to get around, ok, fair enough, but angels are *created* beings....just as man is!

The argument might also be made that Satan and his band of fallen angels who hate man because of God's love of man, would do everything in their power to try and show their superiority to those that they wish to enslave or destroy! Since these beings wish to usurp God by coercing man to worship them, a "god-like" show of power seems like a pretty likely thing for them to do! Although I do not believe that these 'angels' necessarily need such vehicles, it does seem to me that such powerful vehicles could be a pretty valuable resource towards the goal of corrupting man through a lust for power! (Just a thought)

Another thing that bears mention here is the idea that these beings were here on Earth before man. They weren't! Earth was created as man's home, not theirs! (Read your Bible!) Despite the science that shows that nothing living could have functioned mentally, due to the strength of the

Earths geo-magnetic field, even 10,000 years ago on this planet. (More on this in Evolution vs. Creation) The claim that angels/gods/aliens were here before us makes them the heirs to this world, not man and this is clearly not the case. This claim always strikes me as information that was *given* to someone by one or more of these beings! Of course Evolutionary theory being taught as scientific fact instead of the religious nonsense that it is only serves to empower these claims. Remember, the destruction or enslavement of humanity is their goal!

In Exodus, when the Israelites finally settled in their new home, God set them up with an independent government with God as their head. They had no king! Freedom has always been part of Gods plan for his people! So please look very closely at all information that is presented to you. If any new information is contrary to God's ideals of Love, Freedom and Peace, then it is something that we are far better off avoiding!

In *Ancient Aliens* Rev. Barry H Downing, author The Bible and Flying Saucers, makes this statement: "It will strengthen the general concept that our history of religions in the world needs to be looked at with more respect and also with more wonder – meaning what are we supposed to make of this now? And what are we supposed to be doing with this now!" He is talking of course about our technologically advanced visitors!

This strikes me as so very bizarre! This is supposed to be man of God! He even wears a collar! Yet he cannot seem to make the connection between these beings and the god/goddess worship of ancient times! I know that the Bible talks about end times deceptions being powerful enough to fool even the elect if that were possible , but is it really so difficult to realize that when these beings appeared throughout the

Bible, god and goddess worship started up anew, and <u>every time</u> they did, man suffered as a result !

I suppose that if you buy into evolution as fact then it would be easy to look at the Bible as a work of fiction. This of course, is the point. However, maybe it's just me but wouldn't you think that if you believe in God and you teach a belief in God that you would be familiar with the evidence or facts that support your belief? I just don't understand how you can serve two masters! This is exactly what this is; an effort to merge two dramatically different beliefs into a type of pseudo-religion! In essence this is saying "I believe in God but we need to take a closer look at these ancient gods and goddesses!" But I guess that this is indeed evidence that we are living in the end times!

I promise you, that I am really not that smart...so how is it that I can see this when so-called men of God cannot?! Why is it that I can see these connections that seem to elude so many others? I just don't understand this! Is this a result of mental conditioning, aka mind control? Or maybe they just choose not to look at the rest of the story.

The Mayans of ancient Mexico, worshiped a ruler or god named Pacal, often referred to as lord Pacal or Pacal the great. When he died the Mayans built the great pyramid at Palenque around his tomb. Pacal was a giant described as 7' – 8' tall (a little short by giant standards but a giant none the less). Art carvings at Palenque show lord Pacal (according to native legend) descending into the underworld, however according to Von Daniken these carvings actually show him in a space capsule, working controls with his hands and feet.

I can't help but note that the Mayans connected him with the underworld. Yet, Von Daniken places Pacal in the air, doesn't this seem like a message to you?

This program covers ancient cave drawings, art and artifacts as well as some interesting inventions or technology. It is fairly well known that batteries were in existence at the time the Egyptian pyramids were built, they speculate (from wall carvings) that they also had light bulbs. Among the more interesting was a computer which was found to be an astronomical device by which you could chart your position to the stars and navigate your way through the sea. BUT, it was also an astrological device by which you could chart your horoscope! Hmm

This literally shouts knowledge of the fallen angels! This was part of the knowledge given to the daughters of men divining, or fortune telling, (book of Enoch, not included in the Bible) which is a forbidden activity or sin according to the Bible! Is this something that could have been introduced to man by gods/angels/aliens? Oh yes, definitely!

This program claims that the Egyptian pyramids were build to store knowledge, 300 books that held the knowledge of the universe, which were dictated to man by the guardians of the sky.

First off, where are the books? Secondly, this is another culture known for human sacrifice' only in this culture the people are sacrificing their babies to Baal or Ashtoreth. Third, as I discussed in the gods and goddesses chapter, the plagues that God brought down on Egypt through Moses completely discredited about 2 dozen Egyptian deities! {Oh yes, I forgot, the new story is that this never happened, right?!} So, exactly what kind of knowledge are we discussing here?

How important is what we believe?

I am going to bring up Puma Punko in Bolivia here, simply because I know that this is something that will be brought up as "proof" of some sort. To be honest I am not sure what to make of this site. This is a site of supposedly ancient megalithic sized blocks weighing many tons each that were cut so precisely that it could only have been done using diamond tipped tools and machines, and supposedly thousands of years old. These were credited to the Imara Indians, who possessed no knowledge of writing, planning or advanced tools. I am not sure what to think of this except to say that a couple of things come to mind.

One this site was completely destroyed to the point that it could not be reconstructed, it makes me wonder why. Secondly, it strikes me that it could be some type of deception or ruse. I won't claim to understand this, but I do think it's reasonable to assume that no one else really can either! The bottom line here is that we can make all kinds of assumptions and beliefs about this, but we just cannot know what really happened here because we weren't there!

At the beginning of this chapter I mentioned that people were being (or believed that they were being) abducted by aliens. I want to discuss this a little more here.

I bring this up because of a few interesting little pieces of information that I believe would be a mistake to ignore.

Contactee's or abductees', whatever they call themselves have some interesting stories to tell. Often they actually name some of these entities. One of the most common is Ashtar who claims to be from the council of seven lights, this one is particularly interesting since he has appeared throughout history by various names including Astaroth, Ashar and Asharoth, which are all associated with demons or Satanism! Seth, Val Thor and Voltra. If some of these names sound familiar, it is because they are the ancient names of gods! How many people haven't heard of Thor? How about Ra; ancient Egyptian sun god? or Seth; another ancient Egyptian god. I have also heard of people who are supposedly in contact with Isis and a variety of other goddesses and gods which the contactee's usually refer to as angels!

Wouldn't you think that there would be a clue in this? Of course, if you do not read the Bible then how would you ever know the difference?

We would be remiss not to mention lord Maitraya, who many these days believe to be the messiah, often reducing Jesus Christ to the rank of angel.

This is another case of a UFO contactee channeling an entity. Although, his disciple or false prophet or whatever you want to call him, British author Benjamin Creme claims that Maitraya has appeared throughout the world it seems that the press is reluctant to pick up on the story.

Never-the-less, a quick search of Lord Maitraya yielded 17,800 results! I would say that he is growing in popularity!

In an excerpt from UFOs in the New Age; "But what a few pundits have picked up about Creme- whether or not his information about the coming of a new world teacher is true- is that Creme is a long time "contactee" who claims to have been receiving messages and *direct orders* from extraterrestrial beings, whom he calls "the space people" since 1958. And since he began taking telepathic dictation from them, he claims, the aliens made him part of their plan to reveal their messiah and bring to earth a *new world order*. {Emphasis mine}

Keep in mind here that this is the exact same goal of the ruling elite? New World Order, this is the theme that repeats again and again throughout the world and we really need to be aware, of these words, they are vital to humanity and to Christians!

Also, I would like to point out Cremes reference to taking direct orders from them, a reference to servitude!

So who is this lord Maitraya? He supposedly descended in a self created body in 1977 and has been living in the Asian-Indian community in the east end of London; he is supposed to be the world teacher who transcends all religions. He is the Maitraya, the Buddha, the messiah, the immam Mahdi, or the Christ!

He certainly reads like an anti-Christ, but is he? I don't know, nor will I speculate. I do know that the Bible teaches of many false teachers or "Christs" that will appear in the end times. To be honest, I doubt it; he just doesn't seem to possess the presence that the person of anti Christ is supposed to possess. Never the less, he has many followers and that bears mention!

It bears mention that nearly all (if not all) of the contactee's are actively involved in the occult and this fact is very important! I will mention again that many if not all of these people show little or no concern that these beings lie to them on a regular basis! They claim that it's all part of the overall teaching process, and that ultimately they are here to help us! Now, I don't know about you, but I have to wonder why these people think that they can trust these beings to be honest about the overall goal, when they cannot be trusted with small things! Would they react the same way to a *person* who acted in this way? I mean, if a person tells you lies repeatedly, will you really trust this person with something really important, such as your life?

Yet, this is exactly what these people are doing, except it is not only their life but their eternal soul that they are entrusting to these lying, so called *space brothers*! Why??? For knowledge? For power? For a sense of belonging? For some reason this strikes me as some type of addiction, somewhere deep down inside you know it's bad for you but you just don't want to see it!

How important is what we believe?

Ironically this all fits only too well with accounts of fallen angels. Over and over again many of these contactee's call these beings angels, some of these people who claim to be walk ins (supposedly other worldly beings possessing the body of a human) or star seed (alien-human hybrid) actually refer to themselves as angels. As I have already mentioned many have the names of ancient gods or goddesses which do connect with the Biblical account of fallen angels! I would like to mention an account of a contactee in which one of the beings that he was in contact with called himself 'Natas'. Try spelling this backwards!

Do you really believe this is just a coincidence?

The one central theme or message that these beings convey is always either Jesus wasn't who we believe him to be, or the Bible is actually built on lies, or God doesn't exist, or even that we are god and god is in all of us, or some combination thereof, yet no one seems to see the real objective here...why?

Interestingly, many of these people actually do make a connection that these could be demons, yet they defend these beings anyway...WHY? I surely, do not have the answer! I just do not understand this, but then again, the truth has always been important to me!

So, I ask you...How important is truth to you? Does it matter what you believe? I believe that it matters far more than we can possibly even comprehend! I ask you to do the research and really look at what you believe, if the truth matters to you, then please consider that Christianity is what these beings are attacking, it is the one thing standing in the way of their plans, and it is the central theme of their message. Doesn't this tell you something? It should! This fact alone tells me that Jesus Christ is our shield, our protection and our freedom, but most of all...the TRUTH!

How important is what we believe?

The Law of Attraction

Are you being told what to think?

The first time that I watched "The Secret" I thought 'wow, this makes perfect sense'! I knew that to some degree it was Biblically sound. I had heard part of this information before but had never actually connected the dots (so to speak).

Basically put the law of attraction states that if you focus on something with all of your attention you can bring it into your life. The keys to success at this are gratitude, joy and the visualization of the things that you want to bring about in your life. This is of course a simplistic explanation.

In the Bible, Luke17:6 Jesus said; If ye had faith as a grain of mustard seed , ye might say unto the Sycamine tree, Be thou plucked up by the root, and be thou planted in the sea, and it should obey you.

This to my mind sounds like exactly the same principal. Oh, I have heard the argument that this is meant to be symbolic, but this always sounded like a literal statement to me. That you actually can move things with the power of faith!

This can be called by different things, the law of attraction, the power of intention, the power of creation or just plain faith, but basically it is about what we believe and where we place our faith.

Since I started trying to apply this concept to my life, I have encountered Christian leaders promoting similar teachings, I guess it makes sense for Christians to get tuned into this mode of thinking, but the Christian aspect of this teaching is different, more in depth, thank God!

Quite frankly, trying to follow the methods of either the Secret or the Power of Intention just wasn't working for me and honestly, I believe that it's because I am a Christian, I think that maybe the rules are a little bit different for those of us who belong to God. (Although, I really do wonder just how many people this actually does works for and how many are still trying)

In 'The Secret' Jack Canfield author of Chicken Soup for the Soul, says "It took a lot of years for me to get this because I grew up very much with this idea that there was something I was supposed to do, and if I wasn't doing it, God wouldn't be happy with me. When I really understood that my primary aim was to feel and experience joy, then I began to do only those things which brought me joy. I have a saying: "If it ain't fun don't do it"

Before I get too far away from these quotes I want to interject one more here:

Neale Donald Walsch Author, International speaker and spiritual advisor.

"There is no blackboard in the sky on which God has written your purpose, your mission in life. There's no blackboard in the sky that says 'Neale Donald Walsch, a handsome guy who lived in the first part of the 21st century, who _____' and then there's a blank. And all I have to do to really understand what I'm doing here, why I'm here, is to find that blackboard and find out what God really has in mind for me. But the blackboard doesn't exist. So your purpose is what you say it is. Your mission is the mission you give yourself. Your life will be what you create it to be and no one will stand in judgment of it now or ever."

Don't get me wrong here, I am not saying that these people are evil, or even necessarily wrong. I am sure that their beliefs are sincere and for them this is truth, however, these "truths" do not work for everybody!

I would also like to say here that I'm in no way making a judgment on the religious beliefs of anyone in all honestly I don't know what their religious beliefs are and therefore make no slander against them at all. I am simply saying that I disagree with their beliefs.

Anyway that being said I do want to say that I find some problems with this type of belief and I do know that these beliefs are becoming very popular so I want to interject here with this; this cannot and will not work for everyone, at least not here and not now.

I mentioned earlier that this just wasn't working for me and now I understand why. Believe it or not God *does* have a purpose for me. I truly believe that some of us (if not all of us) actually do have a specific purpose.

I kept trying and trying to use these principals the way they all kept saying to, but I ran into a problem. I just could not remove God aka Jesus Christ from the picture. I did try to "hand it over to the universe" I honestly believe that this is where I ran into trouble!

I am not a Hindu! I am a Christian! I am not a Pagan, I am a Christian! I do not have humanist values I have Christian values! So needless to say I ran into a problem here!

I have a personal relationship with Jesus Christ and about 12 years ago I asked God to show me the truth about what is really happening in the world and he did. The problem with asking God for the truth is that if he gives it to you then you are responsible for it!

The law of attraction seemed like a shortcut to get everything that I have ever wanted without accountability to God, without having to do what God wants me to do, write some ugly frightening truths out in book form so that hopefully people can find their way home while there is still time. I know, selfish of me!

Interestingly enough, everything went wrong! Nothing was working right, and we went under spiritual attack. You can say whatever you want about these types of attacks, but I know for a fact that they are very real! Being someone who understands the limitations of what can and cannot be done by way of attack by evil forces on a Christian, I know that I was being attacked from every aspect possible and believe me when I tell you that Satan know every single weakness that you have!

I tried everything I could think of to rebuke these evils from me but to no avail. However, when I got back to focusing on what God wanted me to do, writing this book, then everything began to smooth out and start working right. God wasn't about to let me off the hook on this one and to tell you the truth, I am glad. God has shown me what he has in store for me and it is so very much more than I had in mind for myself! Now I understand what depth of joy and freedom really are!

Anyway, let me get back to some of the problems that I ran into in the law of attraction and power of intention teachings.

Number one, and for me the most important, these teachings seem to want to homogenize God! They aren't talking about God so much as they are talking about the *universe!* Hindus believe that God is the universe, etc, not Christians! I see a great danger in removing God from our pursuits and from our lives! There are a great many beliefs lately that seem really wonderful in terms of short term results but are actually very dangerous in the long run; I believe that this is one of them!

You are making a request of the universe or the source, some impersonal nameless existence that only knows how to create and does so by our perceptions whether good or bad. To me this just seems like a gateway for trouble!

God is not some impersonal, uncaring entity! To be honest, God may be in all of us but only if we choose a relationship with him! Let me ask you this; you are going to have a child, you give birth, and care for this child, give your child everything it could ever want or need because there is nothing in the world that you love more than your child. Then one day your child has grown up and is now an adult. (Let's say it's a son) Now you go to visit your son in his new apartment (that you paid for) and your son says to you

"You're not my parent, the universe is my parent and it will provide and has provided everything that I need, you are no longer needed in my life" Do you agree? Do you then just let him go and tell yourself that he is right and you never see him again? In a sense this is what you are doing when you reduce God to "the universe"

Just as you the parent are so much more to your children, God is ever so much more to us!

God is not some cold, impersonal being! God is a conscious being who created us to be a family to him, how can you be a family to the universe? How can you have a relationship with the universe? You can't!

God visited and spoke to several people in the old testament of the Bible, and then Jesus Christ was born and gave us first hand examples of just how much love God has for us. Over and over God has been sending us the same message "I love you and want you in my family" but the choice is always ours! This is about as personal as it gets!

Another concern that I have about this is the self factor. Yes, I know, you are supposed to be joyful and loving and especially grateful, but your focus seems to be on what you want in your life. Which may be all fine and well in theory but it seems very inwardly focused to me.

Dr Wayne Dyer in the 'Power if Intention' talks about following the path of least resistance. This sounds wonderful, just be happy, following the path of least resistance will help you to stay connected to the source and you will be happy!

See, something that I have noticed in these teachings is that yes it homogenizes God but it also neutralizes Satan. According to this teaching, Satan doesn't exist he is nothing more than our bad thoughts! Or at least this is how it appears to me and I have to say that this is a dangerous way of thinking! I can't help but wonder, if you follow the path of least resistance, or go with the flow...then just how long before you wake up with a microchip implanted in you? Or better yet, sporting the mark of the beast? It just seems to me that this is where this line of thought leads!

In The Secret, Dr Denis Waitley, psychologist says; "the leaders in the past who had the secret wanted to keep the power and not share the power, so they kept people ignorant of the secret. People went to work did their job and came home. They were on a treadmill with no real power because the Secret was kept in the few."

OK, so the question in my mind is, why now? If those in power have been hoarding the Secret all this time, then why is it suddenly everywhere? Why would a group of people who own most of the world's wealth and power suddenly allow everyone in the world access to this incredible power?

Maybe because it doesn't matter or maybe because they can use it to their advantage or both!

To begin with most people can't use the law of attraction, because they are not able to achieve the state of mind necessary to make it work for them. Why? Because we are being kept in an altered state of mind. It's called mind control and the US government holds many patents for mind control methods. That is not to say that other countries don't hold some of their own patents or that these various media are only being tested/used on Americans. Basically we are being told what to think and what to believe by the people in power, so I am guessing that they do not find this teaching a threat in any way.

The other thought that comes to mind is that this group can probably use this belief system to their advantage, because if you are focused on what you want, being happy, loving and grateful (I am in no way saying that any of these things are wrong) then you're either not looking closely at what is happening in the world or you don't want to look because it might take your focus off what you want and if you actually get some of what you want, then it makes it easier to do and believe what they want you to believe. AKA The universal one world religion or New World Order! A homogenized God and absence of Satan certainly fits the bill for this goal! It also removes Gods protection from you. If everything comes from the universe then you have no need for a personal relationship with God because God as we understand him doesn't really exist, no relationship, no protection!

I really have to say that I can't see this showing up now as anything but planned. Especially when you stop and consider the great strides that those in power have been making towards removing God from our lives!

I can't help but believe that this is another powerful end time's deception, which we were warned about. It certainly fits the bill.

The big question in my mind is what are you giving up to get what you want? This seems like a pretty big trade off to me... You get what you want (maybe) and lose your eternal inheritance! Hmmm!

Meanwhile you are so focused and so intent on what you *want* in your life, you aren't paying attention to everything else that's going on in the world or to what is actually being taken away from you! OR, for that matter to what you are being *told* to believe!

The more I look at this "belief" the more it seems to me to be a diversion, the real function of which is to act as a gateway.

This is absolutely a new age belief, centered on the ME, or God is in all of us belief. The new humanism religion is everywhere these days and has staunch supporters such as Shirley Mac Lain and Oprah Winfrey. The belief is this; all roads lead to God! God is in all of us and we all find God in our own way.

Ironically, according to this new age thinking the only road that doesn't lead to God is Christianity! You really need to stop and think about this: *the only road that* doesn't *lead to God is Christianity?* Or should I say *traditional* Christianity! To put it another way you can believe anything BUT the *traditional view or Bible based view of Christianity*!

After spending days and days and days researching this, there is no other conclusion!

The belief in God as the source or as the universe is nothing more than a gateway to humanism or the new one world religion, and this is the point! This belief serves as a means to an end for those promoting this belief system Unfortunately, the best lies always contain elements of the truth, why else are they so convincing? But let me ask you this: If you are following this system of belief to get what you want, how well is it actually working for you? I dare say that if you are a Christian it is probably not working very well at all, unless of course, you are pursuing the Christian aspect of this, which actually acknowledges God as the creator.

However if you are not a Christian and this is actually working for you (or not) then maybe you need to pay a little closer attention to what you are giving up, or better yet to what is actually going on in the world as a whole, while you are focused on yourself, your life and your happiness! Is focusing on yourself and your happiness truly making the world a better place? Or is this just an illusion?

Dr Wayne Dyer, in The Power of Intention, claims that you can't get poor enough to make someone else rich, or you can't get sick enough to make someone else healthy.

OK, but how exactly does the inward focus and ignoring the world really help make this world a better place for anyone but you? Better yet, does this really make the world a better place for you and the people who you love in the long run?

Of course he is referring to the guilt feelings that people associate with having more than others in the world but exactly who does this type of thinking really serve? Believe it or not this is actually a very important question!

No matter what the popular *new* way of thinking says this type of thinking does *not* serve God! (A note here, this is not a new way of thinking by any stretch of the imagination, it is a very old and very dangerous concept).

Who does it really serve?

How important is what we believe?

In The Secret, they talk about the leaders in the past who had the secret, wanted to keep the power and not share the power. Stop and consider who these leaders are!

We are talking about the super rich and powerful families that control 90% of the world's wealth! Also known as the Illuminati or ruling elite! This group worships Satan and feels that they are entitled to rule over all of us which include making decisions about who has the right to live and who should die!

So I ask you to stop and think about the real destination or result of this type of thinking! Where does this path really lead? Considering that the people who actually claim to be able to make this work (and they probably do) are in fact *teaching* this to others, then I have to stop and wonder exactly *why* this works so well for them. Is there a connection? Maybe! What I do know for certain is that, disregarding Satan as our own 'bad thoughts' is a big mistake! Not to mention a pretty arrogant assumption and a dangerous one!

I have to wonder, even if you get what you want, what will this ultimately cost you in the end? It seems to me that the price tag for all of this could get pretty high! Are you really willing to pay with your eternal soul? I'm not!

By the way this is not a new tactic either; give them what they want, make them happy and then take everything that they have! After all, it doesn't really belong to them anyway...right? Make absolutely no mistake here, this is exactly how the ruling elite think and their ultimate goal is your destruction or enslavement!

So really stop and take a good hard look at what is happening in the world and compare it to what you are being *sold*! Yes, I did mean sold, because that is exactly what is happening here, you are being sold a concept, an idea and a belief system!

So, if it really doesn't matter what you believe, then why all of the effort to control what you believe? AND, of course, how better to get control of your beliefs, than through your own needs and desires?

How important is what you believe?

Who Runs the World?

What is Their Agenda?
Who is telling you what to think?

I have been really struggling with chapter. It is an extremely difficult chapter for me to write, because it covers a great deal of information that people just do not want to know or believe. Even though most Americans know that their freedom, their civil liberties are disappearing, very few really know the true extent of this loss and even fewer know why or who is behind all of this. Most American citizens know that many of our political leaders are corrupt but have very little understanding of the real power behind this corruption!

I do realize that some of the information in this chapter will anger and upset some people. I also know that there will be people who will be so offended by some of this information that they will want to stop reading this book, but I ask that you please 1) finish this book, it will come together at the end and

2) Take the time to do the research; it is worth the time and effort to do so! This information is an important piece of the whole picture. This being said, please stay with me here!

The ruling elite or power families of the world are the people who are actually running the world and yes this does include the USA. I have told people for many years that no one makes it to the office of President of the US without the blessing of the ruling elite and this is true. You have only to look at the actions taken by President Obama since he took office to realize the truth of this statement! How many people realize that President Obama went to Russia and told the Russians that the constitution of the USA was dead? How many Americans even know that President George Bush was a knight of England? How many people know what the original 13th amendment (now removed) to the constitution was? This was removed some time ago but here it is;

THE MISSING ORIGINAL THIRTEENTH AMENDMENT TO THE CONSTITUTION

If any citizen of the United States shall accept, claim, receive or retain any title of nobility or honour, or shall, without the consent of Congress accept and retain any present, pension, office or emolument of any kind whatever, from any emperor, king, prince or foreign power, such person shall cease to be a citizen of the United States and shall be incapable of holding any office of trust or profit under them, or either of them.

This amendment basically states that President Bush has no legal *citizenship* in this country and as such cannot hold any kind of public office!

And yet we had a knight of the British crown for a President! The big statement about this was "in title only" this is what was often stated about Bush's knight ship, but reading this, it appears to me that it was the *title* itself which the founding fathers found offensive! If this doesn't speak volumes about the real power structure in America then I don't know what does! Especially when you stop and consider that the Bush family is Illuminati! A little research on your part will show you the connections!

So how exactly does this happen? *AND* better yet how did he get away with it? Especially when you stop and consider how unpopular this president was! Why? Conditioning or thought manipulation...mind control! Think this can't happen? It's been happening for years! I'll talk more on this in a bit. Meanwhile, the ruling elite basically consist of 13 very wealthy and powerful families with an abundance of connections to many more families and groups all of whom are in the worlds power positions.

Suffice it to say that these people are ultra rich and ultra powerful, but this is the tip of the iceberg. They have a shared set of beliefs that directly impact us!

To begin with they believe that they are entitled to all of the world's wealth, including all money property and resources. They believe that they are entitled to rule over us, to enslave us and that the rest of the world exists to do their bidding. They believe that they have the right to make judgments on our very existence.

They worship an angel of light, and yes they do know that this is Satan, but they believe that Satan is good and God is evil, because Satan gives them the knowledge that God denies man. I am of course referring to the tree of knowledge of good and evil in the Garden of Eden. This is of course what Satan really gave Adam and Eve and the truth is that knowledge is power or so these people believe.

This ties in perfectly with the Nephilim (sons of God) in Genesis 6 who taught the magic arts to the daughters of men, and took wives of them. It ties in with god and goddess worship. Nearly every god or goddess worshiping culture throughout history recounts beings who gave them knowledge in return for worship.

I really do not believe that God had any intention of withholding knowledge from humanity it seems to me that the very fact that this knowledge was *visible* in the garden testifies to this!

Before I get too far into this and before you begin your own research, I want to offer you a warning. I can pretty much guarantee you that when you start researching these sites you will have government agencies taking notice of you! Please do pray for guidance when you go to these sites and ask God for discernment because for every item of truth that you find you will find at least 2 pieces of disinformation designed to make your search appear foolish, so ask God for guidance.

You should also know that, according to popular belief, Microsoft built a back door into all of their programs which allows the government access to your computer any time they want it. This has been ongoing for years but the patriot act made it legal.

I had a firewall on my computer (before I got rid of windows and went to Linux), and as I was collecting some of the research for this book. My firewall was one that actually had to be turned on, a simple enough thing to do on start up, but with this firewall any time that you start or restart your computer you have to turn the firewall on. I noticed on several occasions my computer would restart itself (for no apparent reason); I just think this is interesting, don't you? This is not by far the only time that strange things have happened while I was doing research, but I won't get into that. I will say however that if you are going to do any research, be careful. I am also going to say that if you are somehow concerned about government big brother tactics, that it is far too late to worry about it. The fact is that it just doesn't matter. Me, I guess I would rather be an outlaw than a sheep. Anyway, you need to know this, so.......

OK, so this group is basically called the Illuminati, yes they do exist and yes, they are often mentioned in science fiction, more than likely so that the Illuminati would appear to be pure fiction (a fairly common disinformation tactic) as I said before the Illuminati or ruling elite worship an angel of light and have an agenda.

Let's begin with the basics, a little background information. The last several presidents have either been part of or have worked for this group. They infiltrated every corner of government years and years ago.

I am not going to get into a great deal of detail here because this would take far more time and page space than I am willing to commit to this and the bottom line here is that unless you take the time and effort to do the research for yourself, you probably won't believe me anyway.

However, do consider this; The USA was built predominantly by Christians as a Christian nation. As a result of this America became the most powerful and one of the most stable countries on earth. We are the last remaining superpower in the world. Can you honestly believe that Satan and the world s ruling class wouldn't do everything in their power to infiltrate and take control of this power? I dare say that if you truly believe this you are naïve! And if you think that this can't happen here, then, you need to take a good hard look at what has been going on in the way of laws being passed through etc, over the last 60+ years. That being said;

The first thing that I want to make you aware of is the fact that nearly all communication venues in the world are owned by this group. This includes TV, movies, radio and newspapers. They do not have the internet yet but they are working on it, as I said they have a back door through all Microsoft programs. This is an important fact. It means that nearly everything you see is controlled. Keep this fact in mind, it's important. Also I would like to point out that not all of these venues are owned...yet! I do not think that they have TV channels such as PBS and TBN (trinity broadcasting network) yet. There are also some independent radio stations and newspapers, newsletters that are still operating. However the major venues such as ABC, CBS, NBC, most of the movie producers, etc are owned by this group, so keep this in mind.

So what is their agenda? OK, some of this I am not 100% sure of, I believe it to be true, but I cannot verify it, other parts are true and you only need to look at what is happening in the world today, to see this. This is the plan to the best of my understanding.

1. To destroy Christianity/God.

2. To destroy freedom/liberty.

3. To turn America into a 3rd world country.

4. To drastically reduce the population to a more controllable number.

5. To instill and enforce their own one world religion

6. To control the remaining population from cradle to the grave.

7. To seize power, possibly by some major disaster.

While on this subject did you know that the Illuminati members of congress and the House pushed through a bill in 1947 that would allow the US government to take any privately held lands or property with the declaration of war in the USA? They did this by simply waiting for the rest of congress and senate to leave for Christmas vacation and just went in and pushed the bill through!

So let's go through these and see how this list compares to what is actually happening.

1) To destroy Christianity. I think that it is pretty clear that this is on someone's agenda, with the laws and announcements that it is discriminatory to have any mention of God in schools or other public places such as courts or federal/state offices.

I do find it interesting though that nobody cares if they offend the Christians. Any other god/goddess or religion can be allowed in school *EXCEPT* Christ! Doesn't it make you wonder why, if religion has no place in school, why every other religion on the planet is allowed? Do you ever wonder why Americans don't seem to care about this? After all, America is predominantly a Christian based nation and the primary religion in this country *IS* Christianity! So why exactly do *we the people* sit back and do nothing while our children are being taught paganism, witchcraft and goddess worship? Interesting question wouldn't you say?

2) To destroy freedom, is there any doubt in anyone's mind these days that our freedom is rapidly disappearing? 911 did a lot to advance this goal, did you know that there was a lot of insider trading going on the week before 911? A lot of people made a lot of money from this event; it makes you wonder doesn't it? And oh by the way did you know that one of the largest gold reserves in the country was supposedly housed beneath one of the twin towers? What is it that crime investigators say? "Follow the money"? Hmmm

3) To turn America into a 3rd world country. Why is it, do you think that any illegal alien in the world can come to the USA and get financial help, food stamps and medical while the Americans who paid into this their entire lives cannot? Why is it that the systems that were supposedly put in place to ensure the financial security of US citizens has been siphoned dry to the point that there is no financial security for any of us? Yet, any high ranking government (elected) official has a job where they work for 4 years (mostly destroying what's left of freedom and creating new taxes) and then receive paychecks for the rest of their lives for doing this job! All while the American people get poorer and poorer! Ever wonder why? Can you see how this could be a deliberate attempt to break the American people? If not, please read on.

4) To drastically reduce the population, I will get into this in more detail farther on in this chapter.

5) To instill and enforce their own one world religion. For the most part this has not come to full light yet, however the way is being paved with paganism and witchcraft,

and these people are *VERY* patient! [The new one world religion is supposed to be a blend of Hinduism, Buddhism, Christianity (obviously not true Bible based Christianity), Shamanism, Paganism and Islam].

6) To control the remaining population from cradle to grave. It's not enough to enslave you; you must want to be enslaved. Believe it or not they are actually making great strides towards this goal! (This is another subject for further discussion).

7) To seize power via some major disaster. Hmm, did you know that the technology exists to control the weather? Earthquakes are fairly easy to create as well as storms and even global warming! I know that many readers will think me crazy for some of my statements but please do the research! Do a search on chem. trails or HAARP. This should get you started on the right path, but bear with me I will get more detailed.

By the way are you aware that every time you shop at Corporate owned Chain stores you are basically doing further harm to the US economy? Just a thought, of course it has become nearly impossible anymore to find products that are actually made in the USA..... You can make a far greater profit if you work children or the poverty stricken in other nations to death whilst paying them pennies a day for their labor. And if they die, no big deal they can be replaced easily! After all, there are lots more where they came from, right?! Folks, if you do not understand that this is wrong and evil then there is nothing else I can say!

Keep in mind though, that this does play very well with the reduction of world population!

Think about this! And of course the arrival of these big corporate owned chains in any smaller town generally spells doom for many small business owners. Yet it seems to be a necessary evil for most of us these days!

Just a personal opinion, but I don't believe that corporations such as this are in any way good for America, or anyone else for that matter! Isn't it ironic that the people who make these people wealthy aka US citizens are the ones who are losing everything as a result of shopping these companies?

As the recession drags on and on, more and more people find themselves out of work, unemployment benefits are running out, people are losing their homes and property. I had some neighbors who had to sell things to be able to afford toilet paper! Not only are small business entities going under but many states are going bankrupt as well.

I would also like to mention the gold grab that is going on right now. Oh, I am pretty sure that you have seen the ads. "I got $600.00 for my scrap gold" basically trying to get you to sell off any unwanted gold. I can't help but wonder how many people are selling off their gold just to survive. What this basically does is take any real money that you have away from you. This too, is by design. Oh, I am sure that there are jewelry designers that are buying this up too, but I would be willing to bet that a major portion of it is going into the coffers of the ultra rich! I would also like to recommend this web site that I found yesterday, I believe it fits perfectly with the gold grab scenario; http://www.greatgoldscam.com/speed-retirement/gold2.html

This concerns me, a lot!

This sure looks to me as though we are wide open for a take-over in this country. Isn't it interesting that so many corporations are getting *bailed out* by our government, but none of the citizens are! Our government can throw good money after bad to bail out (control?) these various corporations, yet not one dime goes to help any of the people who are actually paying the money into the system doing the bailouts! What is wrong with this picture?

A quick note here, if you know any elderly US citizens who are on Medicaid you might want to take note: I don't know about other states, but in Colorado, if you have Medicaid as even a back up health provider, when you die they will come in and take any property that you have that can be sold, to take the money back that they paid out for you! So you might want to check into this if you know anyone on Medicaid! Isn't it interesting that the US citizens who have paid into this their entire lives can't get this when they need it, without it costing them everything?!

Folks, this is not bad management, this is designed! This is deliberate and they will not stop until they get what they want...everything! Of course, let's not forget the micro chip implant in each and every surviving citizen!

Think it can't happen? Guess what, there is already one in existence for you! Just waiting to be implanted! High ranking corporate officers or people in high security jobs are already "chipped" It really is just a matter of time.

How many people do you think will allow implants to be inserted in them so that they can get what they need, for themselves or their families? The following quote can be found at: http://www.cuttingedge.org/news/n1027.html

THE MARK OF THE BEAST --- SIX-STEP
ATTITUDINAL CHANGE PLAN CONDITIONING US

"Marilouise Kroker: It's already happening with animals. Our daughter, who lives in Toronto, was given a kitten the other

day with a chip in its neck. It contains her name and the health history of the cat. AK: Now, who wouldn't like to have the choice, after giving birth, to have a chip implanted in the baby, with his or her name, yours, and vital medical information? It could even help people locate their children!

What parent wouldn't like that"? Indeed, what parent would not want to "help" their children? You see, this most insidious process is currently being sold on the most idealistic basis possible, tugging at the heart strings of a parent that just wants the best for their children. People are being conditioned, subtly, gradually and invisibly, according to the process described below, the Six-Step Attitudinal Change Plan Six-Step Attitudinal Change Plan."

Something that has had me concerned for a while now is the number of people over 50 who are on lifetime medications! Medicines that they must have and take for the rest of their lives! When you stop and consider that this is the primary group who still understand and appreciate freedom, not to mention the importance of Christian values, then this fact becomes fairly alarming! This is the group who would be the most unpredictable and the most likely to take a stand, and now it would appear, the most vulnerable!

I would like to make a statement here that I have absolutely no intention of rabble rousing here, I am not trying to scare people or create a riot, so on and so forth. My one and only purpose here is to wake people up to what is happening and why. The battle that I am engaging in is not for liberty, I genuinely believe that it is too late for that now anyway. The battle here is literally the battle between good and evil, between God and the Devil.

People need to understand that this IS the war that is being waged against us! You can call yourself an atheist and say that you do not believe in God, but I can tell you that the people who are controlling all of this, DO believe in God. They hate him but they do believe in him!

You need to understand that control of your free will is the ultimate goal!

Now I want to talk about mind control. Did you know that the US government has at least 2 dozen patents for mind control devices and methods? Do the research. Doesn't this fact make you wonder how they did their research?

The year 1952 is when the USA began their mind control program known as MGM Ultra or MK Ultra. This began with a study done by the CIA on how the average human would react when faced by an enemy.

This of course became far more intense over the years. People from the US and Canada became test subjects in mind control experiments. These experiments were done using many different methods including things like sensory deprivation and drugs such as LSD. It is no secret that some of these experiments were fatal. The movies "Conspiracy Theory" and the "Manchurian Candidate" reflect the nature of this type of experimentation. It was real and it was brutal! Unfortunately experiments were also being done using unknowing citizens as test subjects as well.

There are reports of nuclear bombs being set off upwind of towns so that scientists could measure the results of fall out when it reached the population.

Bio toxins and diseases were released near schools and results monitored, of course this is much easier to do now with computers and internet data bases.

Then of course back to the mind control experiments! There is a reason why the US people have been so benign about the changes made by our government. It really is hard to face these changes head on when you are having difficulty thinking straight, when it is hard to remember things, isn't it? Have you ever noticed how much difficulty older people are having with their memory lately? Even people in their 30s and 40s are struggling at times to remember things. Have you ever wondered why? How often do you look up? The big long "contrails" that last for hours and actually turn into clouds are called chem. trails. I know, we have heard this conspiracy theory before, maybe it's time to take a closer look!

Did you know that the number one leading cause of Alzheimer's disease is aluminum? Know what the two main ingredients of chem. trails are? Barium (a poison) and ALUMINUM! Www. ConnectionMagazineOnline.com pg 20 http://xiandos.info/ WHAT CHEMTRAILS REALLY ARE - The Short Scoop or http://exoticwarfare.com/

Of course, there are sometimes other chemicals and bio agents in them as well.

Part of the chem. trails agenda concerns the star wars program. This involves directed energy weapons. I really don't want to get too involved here, but a lot of information will be lost here so please do the research, the first link above will provide you with a lot more information.

Basically, using HAARP, the gyrotron system on the ground, GWEN, ground wave energy network, or space based lasers, combined with chem. trails (Barium powder and aluminum particles, which are zapped and turned into dense aluminum plasma. Ultimately they are trying to create charged particle plasma beam weapons. This system is in Russia, Canada, the US and all of Europe. It is an offensive and defensive system against EM (electro-magnetic) attacks and missiles. They use this method to create 'shells' which can be layered one on top of another for added protection against missiles. Sounds OK so far right?

The refractive properties of Barium make it a perfect medium for unconstitutional spying and the entrained plasma orbs carried on electromagnetic beams can be used for mind control. Basically, these orbs stick due magnetic polarity and frequency mapping to part of your head or body and can be used to carry pictures, like frames of a movie. Satellites can then download holographic mind control movies, pictures, sounds and *sensations* to people through this technology. [The Air force has stated that by 2025, their goal is to develop virtual and augmented reality mind control!] Usually an announcement of this nature means that they are already well on their way!

Have you ever had thoughts or feelings that suddenly appeared and you don't know why? This could easily explain it! For all of you Christians who are reading this, stop and consider this; as difficult as this could be for saved Christians, just imagine how much more difficult it can be for the average person who does not have the protection of Jesus Christ!

A couple more quick notes about chem. trails, as I mentioned before this is an effective way to test biological weapons. There have been many accounts of people who discovered strange substances on trees in the grass, on decks etc, after heavy chem. trail spraying and if you pay close attention you can sometimes see *differences* in trails. For a while whenever I would see a particular trail in the sky I knew that people were going to start getting sick and they always did! I read of an incident over

LA California, where through some mix up, they over sprayed which resulted in many deaths and illnesses.

It also bears mention that there are accounts of sedatives being sprayed on people during the Cuba missile crisis! Hmm. Oh, and did anyone happen to notice that on those no fly days after 911 that they were still spraying chem. trails? They were!

Did I mention that aluminum can be used as a radio transmitter?

Unfortunately there's more, a lot more! Ever heard of global warming? Have you heard about the bees dying, supposedly because of cell phones? What if I told you that 99 percent of what you are being told about these things is (in my opinion) a lie?! This system of theirs has also been referred to as an atmospheric heater and after everything that I have read about this it seems pretty logical to me that this is the primary source of global warming and the dying off of the bees, yes, cell phones play a part, but only a part. But then again cell phones also play a part in the great mind control program, so this is to be expected.

It seems to me that you can get away with anything that you want if you know how to properly '*pass the buck*', the carbon footprint idea, also seems to be part of the mental conditioning that has been ongoing for many years now. Don't get me wrong here, I am not saying that it is OK to trash the planet, on the contrary, I believe that we are just as responsible for our planet as we are for our own homes, what I am saying is that those who are trashing the earth the most are the same people who are blaming us for it!

You might also think about where these chemicals and poisons are going. So much for organic gardening! That's right they are going into the ground and water supply. Don't forget that not only humans are being slowly poisoned but animals are as well! Have you noticed any difficulty remembering things? Have I already mentioned this??? LOL

By the way this would be considered a psychotronic weapon and psychotronic weapons are considered weapons of mass destruction by the UN!

Remember back in the 60s when they started putting subliminal messages in programs and movies? Basically this consisted of putting a message of a single frame with a message like "Drink cola" within a movie or TV program. You don't actually see the message, but your mind does. This made you thirsty for a cola and you would go get one! Everyone thought that these were outlawed in the 60s, but they weren't, which means that they are still being used! This is just one of many mind control tools at their disposal. Did you know that the US government holds multiple patents for mind control? Did I say this before? Hmm.

Now, for yet another uncomfortable piece of information, HAARP's (yes there is more than one) can create earthquakes and can x-ray the earth to find underground military bases, gold or oil reserves. There literally is no where on earth to hide! HAARPs are an ionospheric heater that can be used as an over the horizon or under the water communications system. This system can be used to control weather or create disaster. Think about this, and it's a global grid!

So how important is what we believe?

All of this information, ugly as it is, is necessary to understand not only the ruling elite and their goals but as the major part of the whole picture and the ultimate goal!

Of course there is a lot more information out there, you just need to look for it, but as I said before my one and only purpose here is to open people's eyes to see things differently.

Unfortunately, this group has a problem, Christianity! Christians (true Christians) just don't cooperate with their ultimate goals! Christians believe in freedom and absolutely worst of all, Christians believe in God, in Jesus and we do not worship other gods, or idols! Remember that this group worships an angel of light, so who's religion are they really trying to push through?

Do you really believe that it is unrelated that God is not allowed in school or other public places while we can be bombarded with *every other religion* in the world? The truth is that we are being bombarded, in essence we are being told what to think and what to believe, it just works better on some than others, like say Christians?

Think about this; understanding the ultimate goal of this group to control everyone and everything, if you take into account that the only thing being targeted is the Judeo/Christian faith (and freedom a main aspect of Christianity), then doesn't it make sense that this is the side to be on? It certainly does to me! If this evil group perceives Jesus Christ as their ultimate enemy then this is the side to take!

You see it's not enough to enslave us, we have to *want* to be enslaved and the one barrier that they cannot get past (though they are trying) is free will! That wonderful, beautiful gift from God!

We have been told that the world's population is too large, or out of control, by whose standards? Did you know that if you took every human being on the planet stood them side by side giving each person a 3 foot radius that it would equate to a dot on the globe? That is to say that if you were to take a globe and a pen and make a dot anywhere on the globe, it would represent the total Earths population! So, how exactly does that add up to too many people? It doesn't, unless you are trying to dominate, control or enslave that population! Then, yes this is too many people! Interesting, wouldn't you say?

So, if you want to reduce the world's population, and gain control over these people and you have all of the resources you need at your disposal, how would you go about it? This can be done through a variety of techniques made available through scientific discoveries and advancements, such as bio-warfare and mind control media.

Did you know that the first case of AIDS broke out less than 10 miles from a bio-warfare or germ warfare facility in Africa, which was owned by one of the ultra rich controlling families of the world? It was traced back to a monkey! Hmmm! Of course now Africa is overrun with AIDS and is nicely reducing the population there! Starvation is also on the rise due to failing food crops and military or guerrilla warfare in various countries. Genocide has become a fairly common thing in many war stricken countries as well.

Have you noticed that home gardens aren't doing very well lately? In 2009, in the US, people's home gardens didn't produce very well. Think this is just a fluke? Do you wonder why? The chem. trails that I mentioned earlier in conjunction with HAARP, GWEN, ELF (extra low frequency, transmission), lasers and cell phones are slowly poisoning the water and earth along with reducing the number of bees, these things add up to less productive gardens.

Crop failure in the US and other bread basket countries would go pretty far in reducing the number of people in the world wouldn't you say? Keep in mind that the GRID created by this system is everywhere, including countries where chem. trail spraying is not going on due to the drift brought on by wind currents. But this could not possibly be happening....right? Do the research!

How important is what we believe?

Keep in mind that the US government is responsible for the theory of Evolution (a religion) being taught in our schools and for Christianity being *removed* from our schools! Have you ever wondered why Harry Potter, which is connected to paganism and witchcraft (religions) are perfectly acceptable in our schools? Do you think this just happened? Do you really not see a pattern here?

Humanism is rapidly becoming the American religion and if you don't believe this, go have a chat with school children about their beliefs! They are of course the main target and this mental conditioning is well on its way!

Meanwhile, most adults are oblivious to this conditioning because of our own conditioning, through the combined efforts of various entertainment media (radio, TV and movies), (the directed attacks on Christianity which are designed to make the Christian faith look foolish), and mind control methods that keep you from thinking straight. Generally people are just too tired or confused to really care, this is the point! You go to work, come home take care of your family and then kick back and relax, allowing whatever messages being sent by your TV, radio or movie to penetrate your mind, what could be simpler than this?

The kids are reading Harry Potter? Great! At least they are reading! OK, when was the last time that they were in church? Does anyone in the house even read the Bible? Do these children get any exposure to the Bible or Christianity at all? How about creation science, any exposure there? In more cases than not....NO!

The problem with this is that it leaves kids wide open to accept whatever *new* and *exciting* idea that comes along, which, of course, is being controlled by someone! Don't believe it? Why do you suppose this is?

Do you really think that a power bent on world domination would really neglect the education of its most powerful resource (and potential weapon) the children? This is hardly a new concept! Remember the introduction of evolution into schools back in the 50s! This concept has been known for centuries! If you want to control the population you need to get control of the children!

Nearly everything these days is focused on getting control of your thoughts and beliefs. Why? So that you will do and accept whatever you are told to do or accept! But you have to *want* to do or accept what you are told to! It's called free will! So, if you allow your mind to go on auto pilot, then who does this really serve?

How important is what we believe?

I want to talk about government distrust. This is the very foundation of conspiracy theory, which is why most people want to disregard anything dealing with distrust.

Many people simply do not want to believe that the US government would do these things, and of course the usual methods of discrediting anyone who talks about such things has gone far to help form people's ideas about such things.

However, it seems to me that more and more, people are waking up to the reality that they cannot trust their government. Both of these beliefs serve a purpose. If you still believe that the US government is still about freedom and the individual rights of the people, then you will disregard any attempt by people to make information about the true nature of their government as "just conspiracy nuts". However, the growing distrust of government by US citizens also serves a purpose as long as this distrust can be *guided*.

Keep in mind that the ultimate goal of the ruling elite is a one world government and a one world religion, a global community. Or to put it another way; A New World Order! This being the case, the distrust of the US government by its citizens could go far towards achieving this goal, if this distrust can be turned to their advantage.

Thanks to 911 and the patriot act we have been told that security means giving up some of our personal liberties or freedom and most of the country went along with this, despite the fact that one of our founding fathers Thomas Jefferson once said that "anyone who would trade liberty for security will find that he has neither" we still gave up these freedoms without hesitation. Now we are being told that humanism should be taught and that a personal savior should not, though they are getting a little more resistance on this, more and more people are getting on board with this too.

Every law that they pass takes more and more of your money and freedom from you and seems designed to push you closer to poverty, yet we do nothing and simply allow these changes, because we are told that this is our civil duty, to pay taxes (which, by the way are illegal, Not only were taxes meant to be temporary, for WW2, but there is no law on record that obliges you to pay taxes, let alone higher and higher taxes).

And for those of you who are not paying attention nearly every law that they pass (if not every law) is designed to do 1 of 2 things. Either to take more money away from you or to further limit your freedom. Please bear in mind that after 911 your personal freedoms began to vanish rapidly, while US borders remained wide open. I ask you, if this was truly about protecting the USA then why wouldn't they at least beef up the border patrols?

Yet, people keep pouring across the borders at an alarming rate! WHY? Do you know how many border patrol agents there are in the state of Oregon? One...part time! Does this *really* make any sense to you? It sure doesn't make sense to me!

I can't help but wonder how long before we are told that global government is the best thing for us?! Better yet, I wonder how many US citizens will simply allow it! After all they do have our best interest at heart, right?

Will the world leaders succeed at pushing through a one world religion and a one world government? Yes! It will happen. This is very clearly stated in the Bible! There will be a one world government and a one world religion with a single leader...Satan!

Most Christians know this, why else the need to quiet their voices? If Christians are not put in check then the truth might get through to people and this is counter-productive to their plans! You can call this religious nonsense if you want to, but pay attention to what is really going on before you choose to ignore this statement!

Before I close this chapter I want to discuss guillotines! A quick search on the net for guillotines in the USA will bring you some very interesting results. There are numerous claims that there are guillotines on US bases throughout America as well as concentration camps etc. I strongly suggest that you make this search.

One site that I found claims that guillotines have been legalized in the state of Georgia as their new means of execution, as a preferred method of execution over the electric chair or lethal injection. Why? Money! Lethal injection and the electric chair destroy body parts that can be harvested and sold.

I have not investigated the story but it does make sense from the point of view that the sale of organs and tissues would help failing state economies.

A couple of these sites spoke of the Noahide laws (Jewish laws, by which non Jews can be destroyed), which are a set of laws that have been integrated into US law? By which they can legally execute Christians!

Is this true? I don't know for certain, but there has been talk of these guillotines on US bases for many years now and I believe these reports to be true! Please do the research! It wouldn't hurt to take a look at the book of Revelation in the Bible to see what it says about Christians being beheaded! You might be surprised!

I want to say here that this group of evil people has been trying to push their agenda of world domination through for many years and even though they claim to be 'on schedule' with their *conditioning* efforts, I don't think that they are! My sense of this is that something is preventing them from pushing their plans all the way through. I believe this to be

God. I believe that they cannot finish pushing their plan through until God allows this! Nothing happens that is not in God's time frame and only with God's permission can they wage all out war on God's people!

The rulers of this world do not have the power yet to push this through, but their power is growing and this will happen! It's only a matter of time. I am going to say that I along with many others do not believe in the rapture! I do believe that Jesus Christ will return in the clouds and will take his people. I just do not believe that anyone will repent and be taken after this event! I also do not believe that Christians will be spared these nightmares.

Matthew24:22 "And except those days should be shortened, there should no flesh be saved: but for the elect's sake those days shall be shortened"

Matthew24:29 Immediately after the tribulation of those days shall the sun be darkened and the moon shall not give her light, and the stars shall fall from heaven, and the powers of the heavens shall be shaken: 30 And then shall appear the sign of the son of man in heaven: and then shall all the tribes of the earth mourn, and they shall see the son of man coming in the clouds of heaven with power and great glory. 31 And he shall send his angels with a great sound of a trumpet, and they shall gather together his elect from the four winds, from one end of heaven to the other.

Revelation12:17 And the dragon was wroth with the woman and went to make war with the remnant of her seed, which keeps the commandments of God, and have the testimony of Jesus Christ.

"Immediately *AFTER* the tribulation" This sure does not sound to me like the elect will be spared the horrors!

The thing that the rapture believers do not realize is that Rapture theory and the Nero anti Christ theories were both written by Jesuit priests in an effort to draw attention away from the Roman Catholic Church!

You might want to check out a book called "Could it Really Happen", by Marvin Moore. It is written by a Seventh Day Adventist. The SDA church is a VERY Bible based church! Which of course, is a good reason for people to attack it? But this book is worth reading it makes a very strong case for the Roman Catholic Church as the beast of Daniel! If this is true then do you really want to continue to believe in rapture theory?

What does this mean? It means (I believe) that we are pretty close to the end now and that time is running out! It is Gods will that none shall perish, so we really need to focus and try to bring as many people home as we can. For Christians it is our job to help people see the truth before it is too late.

For non-Christians or those who are riding the fence on Christianity, it means that the time has come to really evaluate your beliefs against the truth of what is happening in the world as compared to the Bible. Is this a scary frightening thing? Yes, but the end result is everlasting salvation, eternal joy and eternal freedom! If you remain in your current ways you will have none of these either in this world or the next one!

How important is what we believe?

A quick note here, some of the people in the following links who provide this information are very angry! This first link provides ton's of knowledge. The site is huge and will likely take you days to get through, but it is a well researched site.

I do not believe that they have all of the answers, but then again, I don't think that anyone does, nevertheless I believe it to be an important site. I do have to wonder why the site is still up, it has been up for at least 10 years, so I wonder. I do have some theories about this, possible reasons why so I will list these here. 1 God has rules, I do believe that God leaves some doors open for those looking for the truth, and I also believe that there are rules regarding Satan's attack on Gods people that must be obeyed. 2 Disinformation, to make it appear as a disinformation site, this site has speculative time lines which come and go, which of course is always used to discredit information, the premise being, "look, this didn't happen like they said it would, so therefore none of this can be true". This is a very common disinformation tactic! 3 They can use this site to collect info on who is actually looking at this site. It makes it easy to locate those who might take an active stand against them! Is all of the information in this site true? NO, but a lot of it is! Please show some respect here, it took a lot of time and effort to put this site together!

Before I close out this chapter I want to mention the Roman Catholic Church; Make no mistake the Papacy is part of this power group! And despite the fact that your research may lead you to believe that they are lost in the background somewhere, I would not rule them out just yet! I will discuss this in more length in the final chapter of this book.

www.theforbiddenknowledge.com/hhardtruth/newworld index.htm

http://www.cuttingedge.org/news/n1027.htm

http://www.thetruthseeker.co.uk/article.asp?ID=9551

http://theinfounderground.com.com/forum/viewtopic.
php?f=6&t=5367

Www.ConnectionMagazineOnline.com

http://xiandos.info/WHAT_CHEMTRAILS_REALLY_
ARE_-_The_Short_Scoop

http://exoticwarfare.com/ www.mt.net/~watcher/nwoquil2.
html

Scare Tactics

Are you being told what to fear?

I want to talk a little about scare tactics that are being used on people. To begin with not all tactics work on all people, so we have a fairly wide variety.

Probably the most common right now is 2012. Is there anyone in the world who is not familiar with this one?

Basically put the Mayan long count calendar comes to an end on December 21, 2012. At which time the planets are supposed to align and bring tremendous chaos and destruction and possibly the end of the world! Hmm, does anyone remember Y2K? There are a lot of people out there taking this very seriously! People are building underground bunkers to avoid this disaster. Of course there have been underground cities for many years and you can bet that for the most part you will not be invited into them, why? Because they belong to the world leaders, it is rumored that the Queen of England has a big one under the Denver International airport. There is supposed to be another one in the 4 corners area, but I have never been able to confirm any of this. Yet, it does make sense. I won't get into what all is supposed to be taking place in these places, at least not here, but the point is made. There are supposedly other reasons for these "cities" as well but like I said. Anyway, To begin with, I am a Christian and being a Christian I understand things a little differently than most of the world. To begin with, there is no need to fear if Jesus Christ is in your heart and life. Fear is not only a sin, but a control tactic! Consider this; if you do go into an underground shelter what exactly protects you from an earthquake that could cause your shelter to collapse in on you? Or maybe a river changes course and suddenly everyone has drowned, or you just plain, cannot get back out because you're buried! No thank You! Unless God himself tells me to go underground and where to go to be safe, I will take my chances on the surface!

Scare tactics are pretty commonplace these days and they are a form of mind control the more that you can be made to feel afraid the more likely you are to give up your freedom to feel safe. This is a well know fact and the people in power are well aware of this fact. To give you an idea of just how long this knowledge has been well known in the U S A, Thomas Jefferson once said that "anyone who would trade liberty for security will find that he has neither"

So, what fear tactics are going on today? 2012 we have already mentioned, a world-wide economic collapse, I know that many people in other countries as well as here in the USA are very concerned that the USA is going to fall and take other countries with it, aliens, declining morals, increasing violence and of course natural disasters - earthquakes being the most destructive, flooding, hurricanes etc. Of course, let's not forget the take over and enslavement of humanity!

Let's take a look at the ways that people are being made to feel afraid. 2012 of course we have this movie out that is full of things to fear as well as TV shows and web info about this 'coming disaster'.

Let's look at this in conjunction with changing weather patterns. I personally believe that the world is escalating that everything is speeding up or speeding toward an end. Will the end come, Will Jesus come in my life time? I do not know! I tend to want to believe that I will see the return of Jesus Christ in my life time, but the Bible says that no man will know the exact time of the return of Christ.

Mark13:32 But of that day and that hour knoweth no man, no, not the angels which are in heaven, neither the son, but the father. 33 Take heed, watch and pray: for ye know not when the time is.

Do I believe that we are getting close to the end and the return of Jesus Christ, Yes! Do I know it for a fact? NO absolutely not, nobody does! This is quite clear and that definitely includes the Mayans!

The Bible talks about earthquakes, false prophets and many other things. Are these happening now? Yes. They even seem to be escalating, but guess what, these things have been going on for centuries! Yes, these seem to be happening more and more frequently, but what if I told you that they may not be *natural* disaster?

Do you think that if the people who want to control you could control the weather or at least major aspects of it, that they would use this control to coerce fear? You bet! People who are afraid are easy to control!

Am I saying that weather can be controlled, yes! I talk more about this in the chapter who runs the world.

Do think about this though, what happens when a disaster strikes another part of the world? Say an earthquake in Haiti or Chile? The word goes out and Americans or other primarily Christian countries respond with an out pouring of money help and supplies. Why? We want to help, we are known for this aspect of our nature. Now is it just me or wouldn't you call this 'more US dollars leaving the country?' Am I saying that we shouldn't help these people? NO, of course I'm not saying that at all! What I am saying is that Americans keep getting poorer and poorer and it is all by design!

Very little of what is happening in this country is by accident...very little. It doesn't matter if it is direct action or a secondary result of an action, it works by design!

Let's be honest now, does a Rail Road car full of UZI assault weapons *really* end up unguarded and unattended in a rail yard in the heart of gang district in downtown LA by accident? And yet this and other incidents such as this have happened! Is it just a coincidence that these are the people who are targeted as worthless by certain other groups? How better to dispose of unwanted people then by getting them to kill each other? I will say right here and now that I do not know if these facts can be accessed anymore, and might therefore be pure speculation on my part. Since certain information and access to this information is rapidly disappearing from public view these days, it is hard to produce the facts sometimes!

You know like the fact that George Bush being a knight of the British crown would have prevented him from assuming any public office in the US due to the now disappeared amendment to the constitution that forbid mixed allegiances within the government of the US.

Anyway, the fact of the matter is that with each and every passing day there seems to be something new to scare us. If it isn't terrorism, then its 2012, or its earthquakes or economic disaster and when one thing starts to lose its impact, then something else happens to refresh the fear in our hearts! Think about it, doesn't it seem like this is exactly what's going on? I often wonder what's going on behind the scenes while our attention is focused elsewhere! A lot of unpopular laws seem to get passed through while people are focused on other things. Please do you research!

There is a great push to outlaw guns, which has been ongoing for many years now, it's interesting how gangs with assault weapons and children shooting children plays so very well with this push, don't you think? Is there a connection? Let's see? Is there a connection between the outlawing of moral fiber aka God in schools with the self centered 'Paganistic' teachings aka Witchcraft with the loss of human value? What do you think? When you remove teachings that value the lives and personal beliefs of others and replace it with the teachings of self, what do you get? My opinion, you get human life that has little or no value! The great ME! I have to take issue with the "God is Me" way of thinking for the same reason. This line of thinking is extremely self serving with disastrous end results! I recently came across an interesting evolutionary quote "If you teach a child that he is an animal, don't be surprised if he acts like one"! I loved this quote!

It is not my intention here to scare people, in fact the opposite is true. My focus, my whole reason for this book is to help you find your way out of the darkness and out of the fear, so that you can know the absolute transforming *JOY* of love! You see, this is the real truth of what being a Christian is all about! Love, forgiveness, absolute Joy and above all, freedom! And it is what the world is really trying to destroy! Christians are hard to control!

You need to understand that the people who are pushing fear are the same people who want to control your thoughts, because if they can control the way you think, they control what you believe, and they control your free will! This is the one gift from God that really irks these people, because they can't get around it! Oh, don't get me wrong, they are trying! In fact they are *REALLY* trying! But the simple truth of the matter is that even till the very return of Jesus Christ, we will have free will.

I am not saying that this makes anything easy, it doesn't. In fact, having free will can at times be very difficult, not just for us personally, but as a parent or a friend seeing someone hurt or destroyed as a result of their own free will can be very hard, even devastating, yet hard as this can be, our free will is our salvation from those who wish to control or destroy us! So think about it.

How important is what we believe?

I recently watched a program on TV about miracles in which they were speaking about the power of prayer. Some doctors did some experiments with virus cultures or bacteria in test tubes, they had a group of people pray over one test tube and not the other, and the results were dramatic. Incubation of the disease bacteria in the tube that was prayed over was dramatically less than that of the test tube that wasn't prayed over. Now that is pretty impressive! Is there power in prayer? I'd say so! It certainly convinced the doctors!

So what about these other things which elicit fear? How about *aliens*? There are many, many people these days that, not only believe in aliens, but have some pretty scary beliefs about aliens! Some people believe that there is an alien invasion on earth that has already begun, others believe that there are benevolent aliens who are helping or guiding mankind who will reveal themselves publicly very soon (as soon as enough people believe in them). There's that word again...BELIEVE! (See Aliens and Angels)

Oh yes, people are being taken against their will and terrible things are being done to them! This is the story right? But what if it is *not* against their will? What if they only *THINK* that this is against their will? Is it possible that they are being taken because they *believe* that they can be taken? I believe this to be exactly the case! AND I am not alone! God gives you power over supernatural beings and there are rules! (Yes they are supernatural beings) If you believe that they have power over you, then they do!

It is interesting to me how backward the thinking of most people is! People are so afraid of these outer things such as 2012 economic, collapse, terrorists, etc. and meanwhile their kids are being taught Paganism, and witchcraft in school, right alongside the evolutionary religion that is constantly telling them that they have no more value than an animal! But *this* is OK!? I call that backward!

There is an ongoing effort to keep you sidetracked and off balance (so to speak) and focused on external disasters and calamities so that you won't be focused on what is really happening! You pass these fears on to your children and friends as well!

What I want to call your attention to is this; What if there is a reason why Christianity is being demonized? What if, the only real protection that you or your family has is actually in Jesus Christ? Wouldn't it make sense that if Satan really is seeking to destroy humanity, then wouldn't he do everything in his power to remove all obstacles to that goal?

Is Christianity really outdated, antiquated, and judgmental or an obstacle to world peace? OR, is this what Satan and his minions *WANT* you to believe? If you do not take the time to find out what Christianity is *REALLY* about then you are subject to the enslavement and destruction of yourself and maybe even your family and friends!

John 14:6 Jesus answered, "I am the way and the truth and the life. No one comes to the Father except through me".

Keep in mind that Jesus *NEVER* lies! And over the centuries hundreds of scholars have declared the Bible to be factual and historically accurate.

Even today, many, many scientists are discovering that the Biblical account of creation to be factual as well! Despite the fact that you will *never* hear about these facts in any mainstream public forum! The earth is not millions or billions of years old...it is about 6 thousand years old!

The Biblical account of the flood is also accurate and if these things are true, then shouldn't you at least explore the possibility that the rest of the Bible might be true too? Given that Christianity is the only religion that is truly under attack the world over, don't you think that there might be a good reason? Especially when you stop to consider that if the Bible is indeed historically accurate and factual, that maybe, just maybe, the accounts of Satan as wanting to control and dominate this world just might be accurate as well? Think about this!

As Christians, it is not our job to judge or condemn anyone! As Christians we understand that a) it is Gods will that none shall perish. And b) the world is running out of time! Being a Christian means that you have a new and loving heart, it means caring about others, as God does.

As Christians it *IS* our job to try and educate people and try and help as many people as possible find their way home to God before it is too late! Why do you think that Satan hates us so much?

You need to understand that in these last days many will come to deceive you. Anymore it just does not matter if someone's story is accurate or factual or not, what matters is if they can *sell* their story! A charismatic person can sell people on anything if they present it the right way! A classic example of this is Hitler! You might be thinking that something as monstrous as Hitler's agenda couldn't possibly happen again, but think again! It can and it will, only worse! I know that this sounds like a scare tactic unto itself, but that is not the intention here.

The simple fact of the matter is that every time you turn on your TV or radio, every time you attend or rent a movie, attend a seminar, take a class or even read a book or article, you are being sold a bill of goods! You are being sold someone's ideas or beliefs! This is a fact!

Another fact is this; *if you do not take control of what you think and believe, someone else will!*

How important is what we believe?

To accept Jesus Christ in your heart, mind and life is to conquer fear! If you fill your mind and heart with God's truth and love, fear fades away and you experience a joy and a love that is unlike anything you have ever experienced before! You begin to understand that even though these evil fearful things still exist in the world, that this world will pass away, but you will not!

All roads do not lead to heaven, in fact most lead to destruction, which is the ultimate plan that the evil one has for you and everyone you love!

HOW IMPORTANT IS WHAT YOU BELIEVE

The Importance of What We Believe?

By now you are probably beginning to figure out just how all of these things connect. What do the theory of evolution, the modern god/goddess pagan cults, UFOs, the law of attraction teachings and the world leaders aka the Illuminati have in common? Every single one of these things are working together to gain control of your thoughts and beliefs.

Are you being told what to think and believe? Absolutely! Are you beginning to see this? Are you beginning to realize just how programmed you are? Don't you think that it might be time to take a step back and examine what you believe and why you believe it?

My sincerest hope is that this is the one thing that is gained from your reading of this book. It doesn't matter if you agree with me or not, all that matters is that you gain a different perspective, a different way of looking at the world around you! It is my sincerest belief that if you truly delve into these things that I have presented here that you will arrive at many of the same conclusions that I have! I hope and pray so!

The truth of the matter is that you *are* being told what to believe and this has been going on for a long time ...many, many years!

Think about the messages that are coming to you through nearly every available media possible. Really begin to pay attention to the number of times within a television program or movie that evolution or evolutionary concepts are presented. Pay attention to the number of god or goddess names that show up. Listen for humanist ideals, the every path leads to God, or God is in all of us concept.{Let us not forget that every other form of evil, such as murder, theft and sexual immorality are also being presented in a manner that desensitizes you to accept these things as perfectly natural or even good, despite the rise in number of children killing each other, in gang membership and in the number of new cases of deadly sexually transmitted diseases!}

Take a good hard look at what your children are really reading and learning in school! Take a good hard look at how many times aliens in science fiction are presented as the good guys while the un-accepting humans are made to appear evil. Pay attention to the message or fear factors when the evil alien appears, Isn't that message always that these beings are super powerful and for us to win it is entirely up to us...there is no God?

Look at the *real* reason that Christianity is not allowed in schools, is it really because God doesn't belong in school or is it just the <u>Christian God</u> that doesn't belong in school? What are you really being told? Pay close attention to the number of attacks that are lodged against every single aspect of Christianity every single day!

I can absolutely guarantee you that you will hear things like: "Books have been removed from the Bible". "The tomb and bones of Jesus Christ have been discovered." "Jesus was just a teacher and spiritual advisor." Oh yes, my favorite! "Jesus is an alien!" Or "Jesus is an angel who doesn't want to be worshiped!" Of course who wouldn't want to know the facts about the real historical Jesus?

How many of these things have you actually heard? All of which make the claim that Jesus was just a man or even non-existent! *This is, of course the point! To make you doubt, to influence and change your thinking and ultimately your beliefs!*

Of course if the attacks are not on Jesus Christ then they are against God, the Bible or Christian followers. We have the ever present theory of evolution which attacks the foundation of the Bible, creation. Things like; "Something in the Bible is historically inaccurate or is just myth, because no evidence has been found to support it". The attacks become increasingly creative with each and every passing day! I have even seen an account of Jesus Christ having been Illuminati!

Of course I *NEVER* read these things if I do not have to. I will read some of these things for research purposes, but for the most part I try to keep my mind clear of ideas or concepts that attack the character and purpose of Jesus Christ. Why? There are a couple of reasons. 1) I know Jesus personally, He is my salvation, my strength, my freedom and my ultimate joy, and I know that these ideas have one purpose and that is to steal these things from me and I will

NOT allow this! I am in control of my thoughts and beliefs and I intend to stay that way! 2) I understand that these concepts and ideas are intended to draw me away from the light and into the darkness, they have one purpose, to steal my eternal soul, this I will not allow!

When you pursue these ideas in the interest of knowledge, you allow darkness to creep into your mind and soul. I know this to be a fact.

When I am doing research, going into these dark places to gather information, it takes a toll on me. For short periods of time these places rob me of my happiness, sometimes the knowledge that some of these people are forever lost is like a stone in my heart! Many times I find myself in tears over things that I have read. So why do I do this? For all the people who follow these ideas and beliefs without even realizing it. For you! For your children, for your friends, but most of all for God! It is Gods will that none shall perish... None! This includes you! I genuinely believe that part of Gods purpose for me is to write this book, to make people aware of the dangers in allowing themselves to be told or shown what to think and believe. This book is an act of love, for God and for you! Time is running short!

The bottom line here is this; everything that you read, everything you listen to, and everything you watch, be it TV, movies, internet, everything influences your thoughts and beliefs. I will take this one step further and say that quite often what your friends and family (and sometimes even complete strangers) watch read or listen to, will influence your thoughts and beliefs as well!

If you allow your mind to follow the crowd in its thinking, you allow yourself to be told what to think and believe it really is that simple! Do you *REALLY* want to let someone else tell you what to think and believe? Are you willing to gamble your eternal soul on it? Think about this. Really think about it!

I mentioned earlier that people often want to use the Bible to their own purpose, to support their beliefs and theories. This is a very popular source of research for the UFO and ancient alien believers, as well as anyone else who can use the scriptures to their own end.

I once heard this quote: "People will believe anything as long as it is not in the Bible" There seems to be a lot of truth to this statement, but I would like to make an observation of my own here. People will believe anything from the Bible if it can be removed from its true context and bent to fit some wild new theory!

There's nothing dangerous about this practice at all, is there? After all, the Bible is just a book, right? How many references have you heard about the Bible being, just a lot of superstitious nonsense, or some type of similar statement? Except, of course when it can be used to support someone's UN-Christian beliefs, then it is OK. Take a good look at what you believe or even just think about Christianity. Do you think that the anti-Christian campaign is working?

What about attacks on the Christian believers? Christians are often demonized as being judgmental, intolerant, hate mongers (in some countries Christians are even being killed!) Or maybe we are just ignorant unenlightened individuals who need to be educated into the new, modern way of thinking, or misguided individuals clinging to some old worn out worthless belief. I have heard all of these notions and recently!

It is actually reaching the point (here in the US and Europe) where people hate us and want to Kill us simply because we believe in Jesus Christ! These people are the minority at the moment but the time will come when they are the majority, because they are being influenced to believe that this is the correct course of action.

Do not be deceived, this is definitely part of the plan. The simple truth is (and us Bible believing Christians have known this for a long, long time) that the world will seek to destroy us!

I know this doesn't seem like much incentive to become a Christian does it? [Did you know that the planned fate of the Constitution believing or freedom loving US citizens is the same as that of the Christians? Just thought you might like to know this]. [Unfortunately freedom is also under attack.]

So why would anyone want to become a Christian when the entire world is coalescing against Christians? Because as bad as it will be for us, it will be far worse for everyone else! How do I know this? Because it says so in the Bible, and the interesting thing is, that all of this was foretold in the Bible centuries ago!

The simple truth is that there is nothing happening today that has not already happened at various times throughout history! The Bible says that it will be worse than it was in Noah's time! We are rapidly getting there!

Whether you believe it or not all of these various so-called "paths to God" (with the exception of Christianity) are leading in one direction, a one world religion that ultimately worships Satan! You will accept his mark and you will worship him or you will die! Period! And there is no salvation or inheritance for anyone who accepts this mark! Revelation

13:17 14:9 14:11 and 19:20 all tell what happens to those who accept this mark and it isn't good!

Think this can't happen? There is a microchip with your number on it in existence right now! And ladies and gentlemen, the only reason that you do not have this implant right now is because of the Christians! The main thing standing in their way is the Christians! Why? Because we know what this is and what this means for the world, we know who is really waging this battle and why.

We know that we are the only thing standing between Satan and your destruction! If you perceive us as pushy this is why, we are trying to help you find salvation, we want you to find salvation, before the evil one can destroy you, and this is his plan!

We stand as a testimony to Jesus Christ and his everlasting love for his creation ... You!

John 3:16 For God so loved the world that He gave His only begotten son, that whosoever believes in Him shall not perish, but have eternal life!

John 14:6 "I am the way and the truth and the life, no one comes to the father except through me".

God created you to be a member of his family! You were created to be a co inheritor of this world with Jesus Christ! Why do you think that Jesus suffered the things he did? He didn't have to do this! He did this so that *you* could have eternal life, and eternal salvation as part of his family! He endured this because he loves you more than you can possibly imagine!

And *this,* my friend is what Satan is trying to stop! This is what he is trying to steal from you, and why the Christians are trying so hard to stand in his way! Of course this only makes him hate us even more, if that's possible!

The truth is that Christians are not "*haters*" Nor do we stand in judgment of others, this is a sin! Judgment is not ours, but Gods place, Gods right and his alone! Jesus Christ is about *LOVE*. To be a Christian means to endeavor to be as much like Jesus Christ as possible! This means that we are to *LOVE* each other, including our enemies! This is the true definition of a Christian and anyone who tells you different is a liar or very much mistaken!

Many people are afraid of the idea of being accountable to an all powerful God. Afraid that God might see their sins, but God already sees your sins! He wants *you* to see them, He wants you to confess your sins and accept him into your heart and soul so that you can be free of your sins! How can you possibly know complete freedom, joy and peace until you get rid of all of the ugliness of sin that engulfs your heart and mind? This is where true happiness lies! *AND*, contrary to what you are being led to believe, becoming a Christian will not end the fun in your life! In fact, when you become a born again Christian, you will experience more joy and peace than you ever thought possible! Yes, your ideas of fun will change... for the better!

Most importantly you will feel clean, how can that make you anything but happy and thankful?

For anyone reading this who is not a Christian yet, but are leaning in that direction, or have already asked Jesus to forgive you and come into your heart, but do not know where to go from there, you need to be aware of 2 things that you need to do. 1) Start reading your Bible, Bibles are available in everything from traditional King James

Version (that would be the, thee, thou and begat version), to the easy to read and understand New American version. This is important because, once again, if you do not take control of your thoughts and beliefs, someone else will, and new Christians are a special target for Satan! You need to fill your mind with the truth, it is the only protection you have against the deceptions of the world! I would also like to point out here that hundreds of the worlds brightest scholars throughout the centuries have studied the Bible at length and determined it to be truthful and accurate, so don't allow yourself to be fooled by the lies and propaganda! 2) Find a church which lines up with what the word of God (the Bible) teaches. Don't be afraid to check out different churches and explore their beliefs. There are many churches in the world today that do not follow the Bible, who in fact, participate in deceptive or false teachings. You need to know who these are to avoid them. Ask God for guidance, he will help you find the right church for you. Church is also an important part of your new life, because it's an opportunity to cleanse and recharge your mind. I have also found that if I have a specific question in my mind, that when I attend church I will nearly always receive an answer, which is generally confirmed elsewhere, and sometimes the confirmation comes from unusual places...LOL.

The world will seek to beat you down and take your happiness from you, having a place to go where you feel welcome and appreciated, where you can hear the word of God and have it confirmed in your heart, is necessary to your belief system. Confirming the word of God in your mind and heart helps you to build a fortress, a stronghold and makes it harder for the enemy to plant seeds of destruction in you!

I attend the Seventh Day Adventist church (for those of you with this misconception, it is *NOT* a cult, in fact I have never attended a more Bible oriented church in my life). I actually received an invitation to a function of this church in the mail! It was a prophesy seminar mailer, and being very interested in Bible prophesy I went and met people, I felt very welcome so I decided to check out their church and have been going ever since.

Throughout the dark and difficult research that I have been doing for this book, this church has been like an anchor to me, a safe place, so to speak. I am very grateful for this church and to Jesus for leading me here! God will do the same for you if you just ask! Allow Jesus to guide you to the right church for you! You will know in your heart if a church is right for you, if you simply allow Jesus to guide you.

I would like to mention that some churches use fear tactics on people. They will try to pressure you into following their beliefs. Some may even tell you that their beliefs are the only way that you can get to heaven. Don't buy it! If you do not find love and acceptance in a church, or if they use the Bible in such a way as to make you feel afraid to not go to their church, leave and don't go back!

This is how cults operate, by keeping you from asking questions or through the use of fear as a motivator. Unfortunately, there are churches that use the Bible in similar ways to the way UFO believers they remove passages from their context to promote their views. (I did tell you that this concept was not new)

I am not saying that the church you choose will necessarily line up 100% with your understanding of scripture, because I tend to believe that faith is supposed to be individual and personally unique. All of your other relationships in life are this way, why would your relationship with God be different? What I am saying is that your church should feel comfortable and welcoming. I really believe that this is what church should be! Safe harbor!

I do want to mention preconceived ideas that people have about church. Church is meant to be a place where you have fellowship with other Christians and develop and strengthen you relationship with God. I do know people however that believe church is there to serve them. To give them food and money when they need help and though many churches do help with these things, if you are going to church with the idea that church is about you and not God then you have it backwards and need to reevaluate your views of God and faith!

This being said let me move on. Somewhere along the line most people have come to think that their thoughts and beliefs don't really matter (of course there are those who want you to believe that their thoughts and beliefs are the only ones that matter, but I'll get to that in a bit) and that our society has somehow evolved into a better more advanced and superior culture to that of the past. Is this true?

Technologically we are more advanced and knowledge is more readily available, but does that make us better? Do any of our modern advancements really make us superior?

Wouldn't you think that if we were really superior that crime would be almost nonexistent? That starvation and hunger would be extinct? Or that people would accept each other despite their differences and be striving to make the world a wonderful place to live in?

Wouldn't you think that greed and hate would have about completely disappeared by now? Or that people would care more about each other than money or possessions?

Wouldn't you think that our entertainment media would be beauty love and joy, instead of the darkness of murder and cruelty?

Does our wonderfully advanced world make us better in any way to people of the past?

The simple truth of the matter is that the only people in the world who truly cherish these ideals are the Christians! But, wait, Christianity is bad, right? Isn't that what were being told?

Even if you are the type of person who likes to watch programs which are full of violence and destruction, let me ask you this; does this enjoyment of violence and cruelty extend to the people you love? Is it ok that your child or best friend for example, is shot and killed or paralyzed for life as a result of violence? Or do you only find cruelty and violence toward other people OK? Because the truth is that when you condone violence you make these things ok in your life! This includes the people you love! Does it *really* matter what you believe?

It really isn't just a matter of entertainment though, is it? The fact is that we have become so desensitized by these various media we no longer even give a thought to how our children perceive these things. For that matter we don't even stop and consider why we enjoy these things, yet, we are to believe that we are superior? Or that we are God and God is us? I don't think so!

And there's the other side of the coin. Those who believe that their opinion is the only one that matters!

I wonder where this concept came from. Of course there have always been people who believe this and the truth is that this idea too, has been around nearly as long as man himself, but in this context, I am referring to the new age ME movement.

This is a state of mind in which you are either unable or unwilling to accept anyone else's ideas or beliefs except your own. Yes, I do understand that this is basically human nature, but as the world progresses it seems that more and more of us are turning to this belief system. Unfortunately it is ultimately self destructive!

You can go through life thinking that yours is the only opinion or belief that matters, but it will end up costing you love and respect, and will result in you losing everything that matters most in life! Is it worth it?

I have already mentioned that I do not believe in the rapture theory. Oh, I do believe in the return of Jesus Christ, the Bible makes it quite clear that Jesus will return and even tells what that event will be like in great detail! What I do not believe is that after this event, anyone else will be saved. Nor do I believe that Christians will be whisked away and spared the horrors of end times prophesy! In fact it seems pretty clear to me that the only reason the end times scenario will be cut short is *FOR* the Christians!

I want to say here that for those of us who do not believe in the Rapture that the return of Jesus Christ has a little different meaning. I often wonder how many Christians draw the same conclusions that I do, though.

For those of us who do not believe in the rapture, the return of Jesus Christ means that more than likely, someone we love will be lost, and that is a difficult thought to cope with! Although, the return of Jesus will herald a wonderful eternity for Christians, it also heralds destruction for non Christians. This is to my thinking all the more reason for Christians to try harder to get through to people while there is still time to do so, because eventually time will run out. To me this is a heartbreaking feeling, that people whom I love might be destroyed! Even though I know that they have to make their own choice, it is a hurtful thought none the less! I can't help but wonder how many Christians actually make this connection.

If you believe in the rapture, then I beg you to consider the possibility that maybe just maybe, you might be wrong. Please take the time to investigate where rapture theory originated! I will give you a brief Outline here of my understanding of this, but you really should do your own research!

Let's begin with a passage from the Bible, Daniel 7:7-8

"After that, in my vision at night I looked, and there before me was a fourth beast- terrifying and very powerful. It had large iron teeth; it crushed and devoured its victims and trampled underfoot whatever was left. It was different all the former beasts, and it had ten horns.

While I was thinking about the horns, there before me was another horn, a little one, which came up among them; and three of the first horns were uprooted before it. This horn had eyes like a man and a mouth that spoke boastfully"

The 10 horns represent 10 kingdoms, 3 of which were uprooted by the little horn. The 10 kingdoms were barbarian tribes which were well established in the Roman empire by the middle of the fifth century (the 400s) The Papacy arose which was a power and *Kingdom* into itself, which was different from the others, indeed it was the little horn or Papacy was both religious and political in nature while other kingdoms were strictly political. 7 of these kingdoms converted to Christianity, while 3 of these kingdoms adopted Aryanism

(Aryan's deny the holy trinity, father, son and holy spirit, and believe Jesus Christ to be a created being and thus, inferior to God) and were thus proclaimed heretics and destroyed by the Papacy. [Visigoths 508, Vandals 534, and Ostrogoths 538]. Whereby they were *uprooted* by the Papacy.

Daniel 7:25 "And he shall speak *great* words against the most High, and shall wear out the saint of the most High, and think to change times and laws;"

Isn't this what the Papacy did? One claim by the Papacy is that the Popes are Vicars of Christ, meaning a substitute for Christ! Or Jesus Christ on earth! Hmmm! The times and laws were changed, the Sabbath was no longer Saturday but Sunday, the first day of the week, which by the way is the day that the Pagans worship the sun god, which is where Sun-day comes from. (You can read more on this in "Could It Really Happen, by Marvin Moore"

Daniel says that he (little horn) will oppress the saints. Is there any doubt that this is exactly what the Roman Catholic Papacy did? Force the world to bow down to it? Torturing and burning as heretics anyone who did not follow their doctrines? The fact is that at one point the Papacy was so powerful that, even Kings did not dare take a stand against it!

Accordingly, the time frame for Daniels prophecy also fits precisely! The Papacy was known at one time to keep people from reading the Bible. People were often told that only the priests had the authority to interpret the Bible. Thus people were kept from the true word of God.

The time frame given in Daniel is also historically accurate. The Roman Papacy ruled for 1,260 Biblical days, which means years. I won't get into a lot of detail here, but the book that I just mentioned and another book "The Great

Controversy" by Ellen White, will line this out far better for you than I could (this book can probably be picked up free at a Seventh Day Adventist church).

The Church lost power (received a fatal wound) when Napoleon's General Louis Alexandre Berthier took the Pope Pius VI prisoner.

The Vatican began to restore its power in 1929. The Vatican has always preferred dealing with authoritarian governments and bitterly opposed liberalism, democracy, anti clericalism and the secular nation state. (The Vatican also supported Nazi Germany in the war).

Is there any doubt in anyone's mind these days that the beast or Roman Catholic Church has indeed been healed of its fatal wound? Is there any doubt that they are once again a force to be reckoned with?

The Papacy knew that the prophecies of Daniel and Revelation pointed directly to it and 2 separate books were written by priests of the church to throw suspicion away from the Roman Catholic Church.

One was the Nero account (used by the church today) which made Nero the anti Christ and thereby placing the anti Christ far in the past. The other is the rapture theory of today. Anti Christ isn't the Church, it is a person! Thereby removing suspicion from the Papacy!

If you delve deeply enough into Catholic books and teachings you will discover some interesting things, such as the fact that the Papacy *knows* that they are anti-Christ! And you will also discover that they believe that the Protestant Church pays homage to them by the keeping of Sunday as the Sabbath! Interesting?!

Make no mistake the Vatican seeks power and would do anything to achieve this end! So let's not count them out just yet. It also bears mention here that a quick on line search for the back pope should bring you some interesting results as well.

I know that I could make it easier for you to understand with more details and greater explanation of the information that I am presenting here, but there are three reasons why I am keeping this information as simplistic as possible. 1) You need to do your own research to be able to form your own conclusions, I don't want you to believe me I want you to search the information yourself! 2) The information is often far more extensive that I could even begin to get into this book! I don't want this book to be too wordy or too difficult to read, I want it to be simple and direct, so that the point won't be lost. 3) Doing your own research will take your mind off of autopilot and help you to think for yourself, so that you can begin to see things a bit more clearly!

I hope that this book will open your eyes to what is really happening in the world today so that you will not be deceived and hopefully find your way home to God while there is still time!

I want to add some links for you, so that you can begin your own search, good luck and may God bless you!

www.theforbiddenknowledge.com/hhardtruth/newworld index.htm

http://www.cuttingedge.org/news/n1027.htm

http://www.thetruthseeker.co.uk/article.asp?ID=9551

http://theinfounderground.com.com/forum/viewtopic. php?f=6&t=5367

Www.ConnectionMagazineOnline.com

http://xiandos.info/WHAT_CHEMTRAILS_REALLY_ARE_-_The_Short_Scoop

http://exoticwarfare.com/

http://www.mt.net/~watcher/nwoquil2.html

http://www.meguiar.addr.com/black_pope.htm

www.thewatcherfiles.com/blackpope.htm

http://www.godrules.net/evolutioncruncher/c04.htm

Young earth

http://www.earthage.org/youngearthev/evidence_for_a_young_earth.htm Young earth

http://www.icr.org/article/earths-magnetic-field-young/

http://www.eadshome.com/Geochronometers.htm

http://www.earthage.org/EarthOldorYoung/Radiometric%20Dating,%20and%20The%20Age%20of%20the%20Earth.htm

http://www.trueorigin.org/helium02.asp

Young earth

http://educate-yourself.org/ps/guillotinesinamerica15feb09.shtml

http://www.texemarrs.com/lucidboo.htm

http://www.cuttingedge.org/news/n1027.html

http://www.biblebelievers.org.au/nl099.htm

http://www.cuttingedge.org/news/n1398.cfm

http://www.bridgeoflove.com/bookstore/icke/magazine/vol14/articles/masonic-33rd.html

www.greatdreams.com/megiddo.htm

http://www.greatdreams.com/americanmason.htm

http://catholic.cephasministry.com/masonlst.html

http://www.bluemoons.cc/planets/daynames.htm

http://www.aristotle.net/~bhuie/gen6sons.htm

http://www.aristotle.net/~bhuie/demons.htm

http://www.villagevoice.com/issues/0139/hentoff.php

Books:

Could It Really Happen

Marvin Moore

The Gods Who Walk Among Us …Thomas R Horn and Donald C Jones, Ph.D.

UFOs in the NEW AGE

William M Alnor (out of print, but I found it easily **At amazon.com)**